THEY TRAVEL OUTSIDE THEIR BODIES

THEY TRAVEL OUTSIDE THEIR BODIES

THE PHENOMENON OF ASTRAL PROJECTION

BY ELWOOD D. BAUMANN
ILLUSTRATED BY DAVID BROOKS

FRANKLIN WATTS / NEW YORK / LONDON / TORONTO / SYDNEY / 1980

Library of Congress Cataloging in Publication Data

Baumann, Elwood D
 They travel outside their bodies.

 Bibliography: p.
 Includes index.
 SUMMARY: Describes astral projections in which people leave their physical bodies and enter a world where there is neither pain nor unhappiness.
 1. Astral projection—Juvenile literature. [1. Astral projection] I. Brooks, David. II. Title.
 BF1389.A7B29   133.9'2   79-24094
 ISBN 0-531-02880-1

Text copyright © 1980 by Elwood D. Baumann
Illustrations copyright © 1980 by David Brooks
All rights reserved
Printed in the United States of America
6 5 4 3 2 1

CONTENTS

1
An Introduction to Astral Projection
1

2
Leaving the Physical Body Behind
7

3
Return of the Spiritual or Second Body
15

4
Instant Visits to Distant Places
21

5
When a Ghost Is Not a Ghost
29

6
A Dream or Not a Dream?
37

7
The Astral Cord
43

8
The Composition and Dress of the Astral Body
47

9
Astral Projections During Times of Illness
53

10
Astral Projections at the Time of an Accident
59

11
A Doctor's Story
65

12
Life After Death
71

13
Do-It-Yourself Astral Projection
77

14
Dangers of Astral Projection
81

15
Children's Out-of-the-Body Experiences
87

16
Some Reasons for Conscious Astral Projections
95

17
Astral Projection in the Laboratory
99

18
The Continuing Search for Proof
105

For Further Reading
113

Index
115

**THEY TRAVEL
OUTSIDE
THEIR BODIES**

1 AN INTRODUCTION TO ASTRAL PROJECTION

Twelve-year-old Sylvan Muldoon was thoroughly confused. Something very strange was happening to him, but he couldn't imagine what it was. His body felt as though it had been glued to the bed. He was unable to move a single muscle. He couldn't even call out for help.

Then something even more unusual occurred. He had the feeling that he was rising slowly into the air. Although the room was dark, he could see perfectly well. The ceiling was only a few feet from his face. His body was rigid, however, and nothing happened when he tried to turn his head.

Moments later, the boy dropped gently to the floor. The rigidness disappeared and he was able to move about freely. To his astonishment, he saw himself lying asleep upon the bed. But how could that possibly be? he wondered. How could he be asleep in bed if he was wide awake and standing on the bedroom floor?

None of it made any sense to Muldoon. He had always heard that a person couldn't be in two different places at the same time. But it obviously wasn't true.

He was both in bed and on the floor and he didn't understand it at all. Perhaps I'm dead, he thought. Maybe I died in my sleep. Or perhaps I've gone insane. He knew, though, that this wasn't the case. He was wide awake and fully conscious. He knew exactly where he was and what he was doing. It was just that he didn't know what was going on.

Gradually, Muldoon's interest in his predicament overcame his fears. He decided to wake up the boy on the bed and see what he had to say. This proved to be an impossible task. Nothing happened when he tried to speak and he was unable to make physical contact of any kind. When he tried to arouse the sleeping boy, his hands passed right through the body. Well, he thought, the only thing to do now is to wake up my parents and see if they can do something about this.

There was now another surprise in store for him. When he attempted to open the bedroom door, he found himself passing through it as easily as a man walks through a fog. The only difficulty he encountered was when he glided into his parents' room. They were both sound asleep and there was nothing he could do to wake them up. Neither did he have any luck with his brother and sisters. They didn't even stir in their sleep.

Muldoon was keenly disappointed. He could move about at will. He was able to see and hear, but he was totally unable to make contact with anyone. He couldn't shout out to them and they couldn't feel his hands. He could only hope that someone might wake up soon and see him in his "new" body.

For the next fifteen minutes or so, Muldoon glided

aimlessly from room to room. A car passed the house and he could see the headlights and hear the swish of the wheels on the wet street. He made one more attempt to wake up his family, but his attempt failed. Nobody could see him or hear him or feel him.

Suddenly, the boy lost his freedom of movement. He was being pulled back into his own room and he could do nothing about it. He saw that his other self was still sleeping soundly in bed. The next thing he knew, his second body was floating a foot or two above his physical body. He remained in that position for no more than a few seconds before dropping straight down into the body he had left about half an hour earlier. There was a gentle jerk when the two bodies came together and he was immediately wide awake.

Sylvan Muldoon's projection was a particularly vivid one, yet it was not as strange as it may seem. Herbert Greenhouse, author of *The Astral Journey,* believes that millions of people have had out-of-the-body experiences. Survey data seems to bear this out. Dr. Charles Tart asked 150 University of California students if they had ever left their bodies and 44 percent replied positively. The late Dr. Hornell Hart of Duke University asked the same question of 155 sociology students and received positive replies from 27 percent.

The most ambitious survey was carried out by two psychologists at the University of Virginia. They asked 1,000 students and townspeople if they had ever seen their own body from a point outside. Twenty-five percent of the students and 14 percent of the townspeople said that they had. Roughly half of those who replied positively claimed to have had several out-of-the-body experiences.

There is nothing new about astral projection, of course. People have been reporting out-of-the-body experiences since the very dawn of recorded history. Paintings found in Egyptian tombs show a second body hovering over the physical body. Ancient Chinese and Indian manuscripts frequently referred to men who were able to send their spiritual bodies on heavenly flights. The Algonquin, Shoshone, and other American Indian tribes believed that they sometimes abandoned their sleeping bodies and floated about both on earth and in the spirit world.

Although St. Paul tells us in the New Testament that we all have both a natural and a spiritual body, there is no specific reference to astral projection in the Bible. Many Christians have had out-of-the-body experiences, but they were not a part of their religious beliefs. In some Eastern religions, however, monks and lamas frequently leave their physical bodies behind and travel in the astral world. Out-of-the-body experiences are an important part of their religious training.

Robert Monroe, author of *Journeys Out of the Body*, says that almost everyone has the ability to float free of his or her physical body. Only patience, determination, and proper instruction are needed. Once the technique has been mastered, the person can often enter a beautiful new world simply by concentrating on it.

The overwhelming majority of astral projections occur while a person is sleeping. The natural tendency, of course, is to afterward dismiss the entire thing as a dream. This, however, is not always correct reasoning.

Dr. Hornell Hart said that if a man feels himself floating in the air and can see himself still lying in bed, then he is definitely having an out-of-the-body experience. He may not even leave his own bedroom, but he is still moving on the astral plane.

2 LEAVING THE PHYSICAL BODY BEHIND

The spiritual body may separate itself from the physical body at any time. It happens more frequently while people are asleep, but it can also happen while one is wide awake. People have had out-of-the-body experiences while riding on buses or strolling along the street. A certain long-distance swimmer said that his second body always left his natural body when he became terribly tired.

A few fortunate people are able to leave their bodies whenever they want to. Sylvan Muldoon calls this "spontaneous exteriorization" or "instantaneous projection," meaning that there is an instant release of the second body. Muldoon himself has had many hundreds of out-of-the-body experiences, but very few of them have been spontaneous. In almost every instance he had to struggle to get free of his physical self.

Ingo Swann, an artist and writer who has often taken part in experiments at the American Society for Psychical Research, is a classic example of instant release. He experiences most of his astral travels while sitting in an easy chair puffing on a cigar. About the only physical effort he has to make is to close his eyes and relax. It's true, of course, that Swann's case is unusual and neither he nor anyone else can explain his strange power.

The second body is often released instantly when there is a threat of sudden death or severe injury. It can often happen when pain becomes so great that it can no longer be endured. In such instances, though, the release is much like a reflex action. It is not brought on deliberately as happens with Ingo Swann and others.

The story of Ed Morrell is perhaps the best known account of an out-of-the-body experience during great pain. About fifty years ago, Morrell served a term in an Arizona prison. Conditions there were more inhumane than today. Morrell was often beaten brutally. Cruel guards frequently forced him into two straitjackets, then doused him with buckets of water. The water caused the straitjackets to shrink, which made the agony even greater.

One night, while lying helpless on the prison floor, Morrell suddenly felt himself float free of his physical body and pass through the prison walls. He had no idea of what was happening. He only knew that he had temporarily escaped his suffering. His second body gave him a wonderful sense of freedom and he floated happily from place to place. The next morning, however, he was back in his natural body, which was still imprisoned in the straitjackets.

This went on until Morrell was released four years later. Whenever he was tortured, his second body would make its escape. In time, he learned to control his astral travels and was able to visit friends and relatives in different cities as well as his boyhood home.

He also amused himself by listening to the guards' conversations in other parts of the prison, then telling them what they had said. The guards thought that he must have found a way to get out of his cell in solitary confinement and they kept a very close eye on him. They didn't learn the true story, though, until Morrell's book was published in 1924.

Many people claim to have left their bodies during times of religious excitement. One particularly interesting case was reported to Dr. Robert Crookall, author of *The Study and Practice of Astral Projection.*

A young English woman was on a holiday in Rome and decided to visit St. Peter's Cathedral in the Vatican. She had been brought up a Catholic, but had stopped going to church while in college. Although she thought that all her religious beliefs had been discarded, she felt a great urge to kneel down and pray. She resisted the urge, however, and went on with her sightseeing.

Moments later, she felt a great shudder run through her system. She recovered at once, but everything seemed different. There was no sign of the crowds of people who had been milling around only a few seconds before. Then she saw them! They were about 20 feet (6 m) below her. She also saw herself walking slowly along with her camera over her shoulder.

The people seemed to get smaller and the woman realized that she was floating up toward the high ceiling of the cathedral. The paintings of the saints appeared so lifelike that she tried to talk to them. There were paintings of saints wherever she went and all of them seemed to be startlingly alive. Even though conversation was impossible, she had the feeling that the paintings were trying to tell her something.

With no warning at all, the entire scene suddenly changed. It took a moment for the young woman to realize what had happened. She was no longer in St. Peter's Cathedral. She was in the church she had attended in England before discarding her religious beliefs. Everything was just as she remembered it. Only the priest had changed. He was older now and he walked with crutches.

Before the woman could ask the priest what had happened, she found herself back in her own body at St. Peter's. Although she said nothing to anyone at the time, she knew that her second body had floated up to the cathedral ceiling. She knew, too, that she had been in the church she had once attended regularly and that she had seen the priest. None of it made any sense to her, but she knew without a doubt that it had actually happened.

When the young woman returned home a few days later, one of the first things she did was to visit her old priest. She found him hobbling around on crutches. He had been hit by a car and both of his legs had been broken.

The priest listened to the young woman's story and smiled knowingly. He, too, had experienced the astral state and he knew exactly what she was talking about. He even had a story of his own to tell her. Just before the car had hit him, his second body had left his physical body. The accident had happened at a busy intersection and he had watched calmly from above as traffic screeched to a halt and people came rushing from all directions.

It should be noted that there is a great difference between instantaneous projection and conscious projection. In the case of instantaneous projection, the subject is usually not experienced in astral travel. The out-of-the-body experience may occur while one is asleep or because one has had a severe shock. In any case, the person is usually experiencing something entirely new and is not certain how to cope with it.

The techniques of conscious astral projection vary enormously from one individual to another. Some people insist that they can get out of their bodies as easily as they can get out of their clothes. They simply think about getting out and they're out. Buddhist and Hindu lamas and monks seem able to reach the astral state almost at will. Others can seldom leave their physical selves behind without a struggle. Success is by no means guaranteed and no technique is entirely foolproof.

Oliver Fox, author of *Astral Projection* and one of the first serious students of the subject in the Western world, claimed that he could force his second body out of his physical body. It was simply a case of willpower. He would lie down on the bed and concentrate with all his might. Every thought was centered on the escape of his second self. Nothing else was permitted to enter his mind.

Fox's method was usually successful. His spiritual body, he said, often escaped with almost explosive force. He compared it to the feeling a circus performer must have when shot from a cannon. The astral state was reached with alarming suddenness, but Fox was always aware of what was happening to him.

The technique employed by Fox would probably be unsuitable for most people. Very few of us have the ability or self-discipline needed to concentrate sufficiently on one single thing. Other thoughts keep running through our minds. Fox himself admitted that he had his share of failures. He experimented with astral projection for many years. Finding a fast and easy way for everyone to reach the astral state was his fondest wish, but he died without realizing his dream.

Unfortunately, those few who are able to leave their physical bodies behind with almost no effort are usually unable to explain how they do it.

3. RETURN OF THE SPIRITUAL OR SECOND BODY

People who have had an out-of-the-body experience while seriously ill or after a bad accident are often reluctant to return to their physical body. They have been projected into a world where there is no suffering. They don't want to go back to the body they have left.

Many have looked upon themselves lying on a hospital bed and reported that they had not liked what they had seen. "I knew it was me, but I didn't like myself at all," said one woman. "I was so ugly," declared another. "I can remember looking down from the ceiling and thinking what a skinny little runt I was," an eleven-year-old boy told his doctor. "I wanted to keep floating on my little cloud," said a young mother, "but I knew that my husband and children needed me. As soon as that thought came into my mind, I found myself back in the body on the bed."

This sense of responsibility remains with people throughout their astral journeys. Dr. Robert Crookall has collected over 1,000 case histories of out-of-the-body experiences. Quite a few of these reports say that people have returned to their bodies because there was still work that they had to do or because they knew that their families needed them.

In one case, a banker floated up to the ceiling during a business meeting. He had been working terribly hard in recent weeks and hadn't been sleeping well at night. His nerves had been stretched almost to their limit. Things were not going well at the bank and he blamed himself.

The banker thought at first that he had dozed off. The meeting was boring and he was very tired. Then he saw himself sitting on a chair at the end of the table. His eyes were open, so he knew that he couldn't be asleep. In fact, he had never been so wide awake in his life.

The situation amused the banker greatly. He didn't know what was happening, but he was happy and perfectly relaxed. There didn't seem to be anything at all to worry about. The men sitting around the table down below looked ridiculous and he felt absolutely nothing for any of them.

Suddenly, the banker found himself at home. His wife was in the living room reading and he did everything possible to attract her attention. Nothing worked. He even put his hand over the page she was reading, but she didn't notice a thing.

The men were still sitting around the table when the banker returned to the meeting. They were a pathetic group, he now thought, and he was the most pathetic of them all. It would be wonderful if he could stay in his new body and never return to the old one.

He knew, though, that this could not be. He had

known great happiness for a few minutes in his second body, but he couldn't stay. His wife and children needed him and there was still a lot of work to be done at the bank.

As soon as these thoughts occurred to him, he felt himself being drawn toward his physical body. He tried to prolong his stay in the astral world for just a few minutes more, but he couldn't manage it. The two bodies were pulled closer and closer together. The banker shuddered slightly when the spiritual body entered the physical one. There was no pain of any kind and only a small degree of discomfort.

Unfortunately, the two bodies do not always come back together in such a gentle manner. In *The Phenomena of Astral Projection,* Sylvan Muldoon describes an out-of-the-body experience reported to him by Garth Rogers of Stevens Point, Wisconsin.

Mr. Rogers awoke from a sound sleep sometime after midnight. His body tingled and there was a roaring sound in his ears. He was trying to figure out what was happening when he suddenly shot up toward the ceiling. He felt no fear at all, he told Muldoon. Beauty surrounded him and he felt at peace with the world.

The feeling of peace passed all too quickly. Although the room was dark, Rogers could see his wife clearly. She had been sick a great deal recently and he was worried about her. If she awoke and saw him floating in the air, it might scare her to death.

"As soon as that thought came to me," Rogers reported, "I felt something pulling me downward. I hit my physical body with a bang and it seems as though

I bounced back up a couple of inches. Then, to my amazement, I turned completely around inside my body. It was the strangest sensation I had ever experienced. It all happened so fast, though, that I didn't even have time to be frightened."

Many of the people interviewed by Celia Green for her book *Out-of-the-Body Experiences* described how their second body rejoined their physical body. In some cases, the two bodies came together with a sharp jolt. This usually happened when the second body was brought back suddenly from a great distance. It happened, too, when the second body was frightened by something.

One woman said that her spiritual body had simply floated into the body on the bed. Another said that the two bodies had glided together, and one used the word *melted*. A university student who projected frequently said that her second body sometimes dived into her physical body and sometimes crawled into it. Others said that their floating body simply lay down in their physical body.

Sylvan Muldoon was one of the very few astral projectors who could control the return of his spiritual body. He always began his astral journeys while lying flat on his back. After years of experimenting, he finally developed the ability to return by letting his second body float above his physical body in exactly the same position. The two bodies then simply melted back into one.

It must be remembered, of course, that Muldoon had had many hundreds of out-of-the-body experiences during the course of his lifetime. The rest of us probably wouldn't have much luck with his method. It proves, though, that the return of the second body actually can be controlled.

4 INSTANT VISITS TO DISTANT PLACES

Dr. Robert Crookall and other writers say that astral projectors can sometimes travel anywhere at the "speed of thought." Ingo Swann is an excellent example of this. Swann has taken part in experiments for the American Society for Psychical Research, the City College of New York, and at Stanford Research Institute in California, and the results have always been the same: he has left the scientists shaking their heads in amazement.

Swann was born in Colorado in 1933. As a boy he would leave his body and zoom deep down into the earth. At other times, he would visit the more exotic parts of the globe. He was able to travel in his spiritual body simply by thinking about it, but it just never occurred to him that he possessed any exceptional powers.

It was while working for the United Nations in New York that Swann first became interested in parapsychology. He eventually contacted the American Society for Psychical Research. The staff realized at once that their visitor was a most remarkable man. At that time, the Society was attempting to prove that out-of-the-body experiences were a scientific fact and they invited Swann to assist them in their experiments.

In the first series of experiments, Swann was asked to draw pictures of certain objects he was not able to see. He was to enter his second body, then float up to a platform suspended from the ceiling. The objects he was to draw were hidden behind a partition on the platform. There was no possible way that he could have seen them while in his physical body.

The results were always gratifying, but they were better on some days than others. Strangely enough, Swann was able to predict his good days. Before the experiments began, he would enter his second body to test its vision. He would then tell the staff how he expected to score.

The staff at the American Society for Psychical Research found Swann an excellent subject. He had trained himself to leave his physical body anywhere and at any time. The great majority of his out-of-the-body experiences took place while he was fully awake. He was able to tell the researchers when he was going to leave his body and also the exact moment of his return.

While working with Janet Mitchell, a research assistant at the American Society for Psychical Research, Swann discovered that he could go out of his body upon command. He could also return the same way. If Miss Mitchell ordered his second body to leave his physical body, it left at once. It returned the very second that the researcher ordered it to. By measuring Swann's brain wave patterns, Miss Mitchell could always tell when Swann was out of his body.

23 INSTANT VISITS TO DISTANT PLACES

Although Swann enjoyed his fourteen months at the American Society for Psychical Research, he found the experiments at the Stanford Research Institute more challenging. In one series, he was given the latitudes and longitudes of certain places on the globe. His instructions were to go to the spot while out of his body, then describe the place that he had visited.

Ingo Swann would immediately leave his physical body and his astral body would travel to the designated spot instantly. When his two bodies were again joined together, he would sketch the mountains, rivers, roads, and buildings he had seen there. Once again, the successes far outnumbered the failures.

One of the early experiments took a rather amusing turn. Swann had journeyed astrally to a tiny, remote island in the southern part of the Indian Ocean. He carefully sketched what he saw there, then told the researchers that he had heard people speaking French. This seemed strange. The atlases and reference books said that the island was uninhabited and always had been. Then someone made an interesting discovery: the French Government had recently built a meteorological station on the island and a number of French technicians were manning it.

In 1973, Swann got bored after months of experiments at Stanford Research Institute. He thought that a trip would do him good and he decided to pay a visit to the planet Jupiter. The fact that this meant a journey of 600 million miles (965 million km) didn't worry him in the least. Distance was something that didn't bother Swann. He would be on the planet as soon as he thought about it.

25 INSTANT VISITS TO DISTANT PLACES

It was actually more than boredom or a mere whim that prompted the project. Astronomy was one of Swann's interests and he knew that NASA's Pioneer 10 spacecraft would bypass the distant planet in about nine months. The craft would send back data on Jupiter and he wanted to see how the data would compare with his own observations.

Swann left California for Jupiter at 6:00 P.M. on April 27, 1973. When he returned from his 600-million mile (965 million km) two-way journey half an hour later, his description of the planet was recorded by Dr. Harold Puthoff and Dr. Russell Targ. One copy of the recordings was kept in a safe at Stanford Research Institute. Other copies were sent to NASA and to several famous astrophysicists.

On December 3, 1973, Pioneer 10 began sending back data on Jupiter. To the amazement of the scientists, the data was remarkably similar to that recorded by Swann after his astral journey. "Swann's description of the planet's atmospheric conditions states nothing that differs to any degree from the Pioneer 10 data," declared one astrophysicist. Another put it more strongly: "We have learned more about Jupiter from the psychic at Stanford than we have from Pioneer 10," he stated.

The science editor of a well-known national magazine was not at all impressed by Swann's achievement. He refused to believe that Swann had gone to a distant planet in his second body. His observations were lucky guesses based upon what astrophysicists and astronomers believed to be true of Jupiter, he said.

Then the science editor issued a challenge: Mariner 10, another spacecraft, was scheduled to send back data on the planet Mercury on March 29, 1974. Very little was known about Mercury and the editor challenged Swann to travel there astrally and record his observations before Mariner 10 bypassed the planet.

It was the sort of challenge Swann liked. Almost all he knew about Mercury was that it was 36 million miles (58 million km) from the sun. He was anxious to learn more about the planet and he scheduled his trip for 9:00 P.M. on March 11, 1974.

Janet Mitchell of the American Society for Psychical Research was asked to monitor the experiment and record the observations. One copy of Swann's description of the planet was to be kept at the research office. Other copies were to be sent to NASA, various astrophysicists, the Central Premonitions Registry in New York and the science editor whose challenge had prompted Swann to make the journey.

The scientists who read Swann's report didn't quite know what to think. It did not agree at all with what they had always believed to be a true picture of Mercury. Swann said that the planet had both a magnetic field and a thin atmosphere. Astrophysicists and astronomers were of the opinion that neither one of these were present on the planet. There was no way to disprove the report, however, until they received the data that would be radioed back by Mariner 10.

The data arrived less than three weeks later. The scientists studied it and could hardly believe what they were seeing. Ingo Swann was right! The planet Mercury had both an atmosphere and a magnetic field.

27 INSTANT VISITS TO DISTANT PLACES

There could be absolutely no doubt about that. Mariner 10 confirmed everything that Swann had said.

It must be admitted that Ingo Swann's astral journeys are not typical out-of-the-body experiences. Sylvan Muldoon, for example, said, "The places I visit during my astral excursions are almost invariably places well known to me. Although I have occasionally been transported to distant scenes and distant lands, it is rare indeed that I am transported into any of the astral realms."

Swann and Muldoon, of course, have both had innumerable out-of-the-body experiences. They can usually control the flight of the second body, but others have very little control or none at all. They may travel only a block from their physical bodies while in the astral state or they may travel thousands or even millions of miles. The second body, it seems, has a mind of its own and is not always cooperative. Muldoon sometimes found himself in places where he didn't want to be and this has happened to others as well.

Another very gifted astral projector is Alex Tanous of Portland, Maine. Like Ingo Swann, Tanous can project at will and his travels will take him anywhere. Tanous, too, has taken part in experiments at the American Society for Psychical Research. He sometimes amuses himself by going there in his spiritual body to see what's happening. He also hopes that some of the staff will see his second body and this has actually happened on at least one occasion.

One of Tanous's most dramatic projections took place while being interviewed during the Vietnam War on the "Maine-Line" program of WGAN in Portland. A young woman phoned the station to ask for help. Her husband was a soldier in Vietnam and she hadn't heard from him for some time. Was there anything Tanous could do? she wanted to know.

"I'll have to go there," Tanous said over the air.

Thousands of listeners waited anxiously to see what would happen. Fortunately, they didn't have to wait long at all. Tanous was back on "Maine-Line" just a few moments later and he had good news for the young wife. Her husband had been transferred to another army post, he told her, and she would hear from him very soon. There was nothing to worry about.

The soldier's wife phoned Tanous the next day. She had just received a letter from her husband. He had recently been moved to another camp and hadn't had time to write.

"But how could you possibly have known these things?" she inquired.

That was one question that Alex Tanous could not answer. He was able to do many extraordinary things, but he could not explain how he did them.

5 WHEN A GHOST IS NOT A GHOST

There are times when a person can be seen by others while having an out-of-the-body experience. When this happens, the astral projector in a sense becomes the ghost of himself or herself. He or she may or may not be recognized, but people may be aware that they have been visited by a spirit of some type.

Nobody has yet been able to explain this satisfactorily. The astral projector is usually completely conscious. They know that they have left their physical body behind and are now in the spiritual body. They can see themselves, but have no way of knowing whether or not this might be one of the times when they can also be seen by others.

It sometimes happens that one person in a room will see a ghost and others in the same room will see nothing. Researchers try to explain this by saying that some people are more psychic than others. This is undoubtedly true and there are many case histories which support this theory. In some instances, even the identity of the ghost was established.

Husbands and wives frequently project to one another. In one highly unusual case, however, a wife projected herself far out to sea and was seen by both her husband and his cabinmate. Known as the famous Wilmot case, it has been carefully investigated by the British Society for Psychical Research.

The year was 1862 and Mr. Wilmot was coming home from England by ship. It was the middle of winter, and the Atlantic was lashed by storms. Wilmot was asleep in his bunk one morning when he dreamed that his wife had entered his stateroom. She was wearing only a nightdress and her long hair was hanging loosely down her back. Before she reached his bunk, she hesitated for a moment and looked around her. Then she bent down, kissed him gently on the lips, and disappeared.

Wilmot woke up to the sound of laughter. "You're really quite a guy," chuckled his cabinmate in the upper bunk. "Having a lady come to visit you like that at this time of the morning." The event may have seemed like a dream to Wilmot. His cabinmate, though, had been wide awake and had clearly seen the ghost of Mrs. Wilmot.

When Wilmot arrived at his home in Bridgeport, Connecticut, his wife asked him if he had received an early morning visit from her a week earlier. Wilmot replied that they had then been more than 1,000 miles (1,600 km) out to sea.

His wife said that she had been terribly worried about him and could not get to sleep. At 4:00 A.M., she left her body and floated out over the ocean. She landed on a steamship and walked along the deck until she came to his stateroom. The man in the upper bunk was awake and he had looked directly into her eyes. After hesitating for a moment, she bent down and

kissed her husband on the lips. She was then pulled back immediately to her bed in Bridgeport.

There seems little doubt but that Mrs. Wilmot actually did visit her husband while in her second body. Her description of the stateroom was accurate in every respect. She had even noticed that the upper bunk was set back some distance from the lower. The cabinmate had said that the visitor had hesitated a moment before kissing Wilmot and Mrs. Wilmot confirmed this. Every detail had occurred to Wilmot in his dream. He had even felt his wife's kiss on his lips.

In *More Astral Projections,* Dr. Robert Crookall tells about a case where a young English woman actually carried on a conversation with a ghost. The incident was described in a letter from the young woman's mother. As in the Wilmot case, the visit took place on board a ship.

The daughter had recently married an American and was on her way to her new home in the United States. She had always been very close to her mother and missed her greatly. The mother also missed her daughter and wondered if she would ever see her again.

One afternoon, the mother was sitting in an armchair thinking about her daughter. The next thing she knew, she was aboard a ship sitting on her daughter's bunk. The young woman was terribly alarmed at first. She knew that the visitor was her mother, but couldn't understand how she had gotten aboard a ship in the middle of the Atlantic Ocean. Her fears passed, however, when her mother took her hand and began talking to her in a soft and soothing voice.

33 WHEN A GHOST IS NOT A GHOST

The letter intrigued Crookall and he asked the mother for more details. He was particularly interested in knowing whether an actual conversation had taken place. The mother replied that no words had actually been spoken. The conversation took place by thought transference. Crookall next wrote to the daughter who confirmed that everything had happened exactly as her mother had described it.

A few astral projectors are always recognized and Hereward Carrington tells about one such case in *Higher Psychical Development.* A woman he knew personally would frequently visit friends in other parts of the country during her out-of-the-body experiences. For reasons which Carrington was unable to explain, her spiritual body was immediately recognized. Her unexpected visits were a source of great worry and distress to her friends. They naturally assumed that she had died and that they were seeing her ghost. No matter how often she visited her friends, they could never become accustomed to her ghostly presence.

People are normally not frightened by the ghosts of people having an out-of-the-body experience. There is a strong tendency for the ghost to visit only friends or relatives. If the ghost happens to be seen, the people who do see it will most likely be more worried than afraid. They will naturally assume that they are seeing the spirit of their dead relative or friend. Unless they know that the person is an astral projector, they will have no way of knowing that his or her physical body is safe at home in bed.

The English astral projector, Oliver Fox, became

quite a nuisance. His college sweetheart was called Elsie and he frequently projected to her bedroom where she was always able to see him. Elsie wasn't at all in favor of the nightly visits.

The visits finally provoked a lovers' quarrel. Fox told Elsie that she didn't know anything about astral projection and she said that she knew as much about it as he did. "And I'll prove it!" she exclaimed. "It's wicked, but I don't care. I'll come to your room tonight and visit you."

"All right," Fox laughed. "Come if you can."

Fox tells what happened in his book, *Astral Projection:*

> I went to bed late and very tired. Elsie's boast had seemed so childish that I never even gave it a thought. It was ridiculous to suppose that she could project herself to my bedroom on her first attempt. A successful astral projection just isn't that easy.
>
> I awoke sometime during the night. I could hear the clock ticking and dimly see the objects in the room. Suddenly, there appeared an egg-shaped cloud of intensely brilliant bluish-white light. In the middle was Elsie, her hair hanging loose. She seemed perfectly solid as she stood by a chest of drawers near the right-hand side of my bed. She looked at me calmly, but made no effort to speak.
>
> For what seemed to be some seconds, I could not move or utter a word. Wonder and admiration filled me, but I was not afraid of her. At last I broke

the spell. Rising on one elbow, I called her name. She then vanished as suddenly as she had come.

We met the following evening and I found Elsie very excited and triumphant. "I did come to you!" she exclaimed. "I really did. I went to sleep willing that I would and all at once I was there."

To his great disgust, nobody believed Fox's story. Even his best friends gave him odd looks when he told them about his experience.

The year was 1905, and astral projection was not yet a respectable topic.

6 A DREAM OR NOT A DREAM?

Webster's New Collegiate Dictionary defines a dream as "A series of thoughts, images or emotions occurring during sleep; any seeming of reality occurring to one sleeping."

Researchers often run into problems with the people they interview because it is sometimes difficult to tell whether they are describing an out-of-the-body experience or a particularly vivid dream. As everyone knows, a dream can seem frighteningly real. An astral projection, on the other hand, not only seems real—it *is* real to the person involved. The person may be asleep when it happens, but he or she often becomes conscious after leaving his or her physical body.

Herbert Greenhouse says that there is one way to tell the difference between an astral projection and a dream. If people are able to see their physical body, they can be fairly certain that they are having an out-of-the-body experience. Greenhouse, however, hurriedly adds that this rule doesn't always work. In the case of a spontaneous projection there is usually no time to look back at your sleeping form. You may be projected straight from your bed to a distant land and be returned almost as suddenly.

Many astral voyagers say that they often project while dreaming. Some even claim that they are able to step into their dream and actually become a part of it while fully conscious. It is entirely possible, they insist, to plan your dream before you fall asleep. You simply concentrate on the person, place, or event with all your power. Everything else must be forced out of your mind. A bit of consciousness still remains when the dream begins and it is then that the projector must leave his or her physical self.

An interesting combination of dreams and out-of-the-body experiences was reported to the British Society for Psychical Research. An English couple became interested in astral projection and decided to experiment with it. They tried and tried, but nothing ever happened. They simply could not get out of their bodies.

A few months after the first experiments, the husband was given a temporary assignment in Holland. His wife was unable to accompany him, but they made plans to meet in the astral state. They would decide on a time, then try to leave their bodies at the appointed hour.

The wife was successful on her very first attempt. She lay down and concentrated on her husband, believing that he was concentrating on her at the same time. She was hovering somewhere between consciousness and unconsciousness when she felt herself rising slowly into the air. *I did it!* she remembers thinking. *I've broken free.* In practically the same instant, she appeared in her husband's hotel room in her second body. He was sound asleep and snoring loudly.

For what seemed like a very long time, she stood looking down at him. When she finally tried to wake him up, however, she was unable to do so. Her hands were the hands of a ghost and he felt absolutely nothing. *Oh well,* she thought. *I'll just let him sleep.*

She was looking idly around the room when her husband suddenly sat straight up in bed. "Muriel," he called out. "Is that you, Muriel?"

Before the wife could even attempt to communicate with her husband, she was drawn back into her own bedroom. The reunion of the two bodies awakened her and she immediately phoned her husband. "It worked!" she exclaimed excitedly. "It worked! I saw you just as plain as day."

"What worked?" Her husband's voice was heavy with sleep. "What are you talking about, darling? Are you all right?"

"I projected to you," she said. "I came to your bedroom and you saw me. You even called out to me."

Unfortunately, both dreams and out-of-the-body experiences are easily forgotten. The husband explained that he had had a tough day. He had gone to bed early and fallen asleep at once. He couldn't remember whether he had dreamed or not, but he was quite sure that he hadn't seen anyone in his room.

Although his wife was disappointed, she wanted the experiments to continue. They agreed to make another attempt a week later. The woman was again successful. She floated free of her physical form and found herself standing beside her husband's bed. Whether or not he was asleep, she couldn't be sure. She would just have to wait and see what happened.

Loud voices in the corridor of the hotel forced the woman back into her own body a moment later. She lay quietly in bed thinking about her astral journey. The experience had thrilled her so much that she was afraid she wouldn't be able to sleep. Finally, she got up and took a sleeping pill. She had to go to work in the morning and she needed her rest.

Sometime later, she felt the presence of another person in her bedroom. Somebody was standing beside her dresser and she knew that it could only be her husband. He had finally managed to reach her in his second body. I'll have to be very quiet, she whispered to herself, or I'll scare him away. I don't dare say a word.

The two stared at one another for what seemed like a full minute. Then the ghost walked over to the bed, kissed his wife on the cheek and disappeared. The woman jumped out of bed at once and dialed her husband's number in Holland. "I saw you!" she practically shouted into the phone. "I could see you perfectly!"

The husband patiently explained that he had been sound asleep for nearly five hours. He had concentrated on her at the set time, but nothing had happened. Loud voices in the corridor had disturbed him, but he had fallen asleep shortly thereafter. He felt certain that he hadn't dreamed and positive that he hadn't had an out-of-the-body experience.

This case is particularly baffling. One researcher thinks that the sleeping pill taken by the wife may have induced a hallucination. He then adds that it was most likely nothing more than a vivid dream. Another says it's possible that the husband actually did leave his body without being aware of it. People have, in fact, appeared in front of others in their second body and known nothing about it until they were told later. This happens quite frequently to Stuart Harary, a staff member at the Psychical Research Foundation in Durham, North Carolina.

The wife's out-of-the-body experiences certainly seem genuine enough. She accurately described everything in her husband's hotel room. Her first successful astral projection delighted her so much that she impulsively telephoned her husband. Her second was so thrilling that she couldn't sleep without taking a pill. The loud voices both she and her husband heard in the corridor also may be taken as proof that she was actually there. There's no way of knowing, of course, whether or not the husband would have seen his wife's ghost if he had been awake at the time of her visits.

Neither is there any way of knowing for certain whether the husband had an out-of-the-body experience or whether his wife had a dream.

7 THE ASTRAL CORD

One of the many confusing things about astral projection is the astral cord. It connects the two bodies and seems to be composed of the same substance as the spiritual body. It cannot be broken or torn and can be stretched out forever and ever.

The most simple definition of the astral cord is given by Herbert Greenhouse in *The Book of Psychic Knowledge:*

> The astral cord has been variously described by astral travelers as a ribbon-like strand, a silky thread, a cord, or an elastic cable, surrounded by light and connected to the head of the physical body. It is about two or three inches thick when the two bodies are close together, but it becomes thinner as the astral body moves farther away. The cord is indestructible and will stretch out interminably. At death, however, the cord is severed from the physical body. There appears to be no danger that this will happen accidentally during an out-of-the-body experience.

Nearly every writer on astral projection mentions the astral cord. The reader quickly assumes that anyone who travels on the astral plane is aware of this connection between the two bodies, but this isn't the case at all. Dr. Robert Crookall found that 22 percent of the first 250 case histories of out-of-the-body experiences which he collected mentioned this connecting link. On the other hand, Celia Green's survey showed that only 3 out of a 100 of those people claiming to have left their bodies said that they had seen something stretched between their second body and their natural body. Thirty percent said, however, that their bodies felt connected in some way.

Muldoon has an explanation for this. When people enter the astral state, he says, they enter a different dimension. It is unlike anything they have ever experienced before and they are totally absorbed in what they see. They are so absorbed that they pay little or no attention to their second body. Then, too, they may have projected themselves a considerable distance. In that case, the astral cord might be no thicker than a single strand of cobweb and would hardly be noticeable. Moreover, the astral cord would be attached to the back of the head and one would have to turn around to see it.

The closer the spiritual body is to the physical body, the greater the thickness of the astral cord. Muldoon says that at a distance of 6 feet (1.83 m), the cord itself is about 6 inches (15 cm) around. It appears to be larger, though, because it is surrounded by an aura of light. This aura gradually disappears as the distance between the two bodies increases.

THE ASTRAL CORD

When a person has a conscious or voluntary out-of-the-body experience, the astral cord can have a tremendous effect on the phantom body. The projector often has to struggle to get free of the physical self. The pull becomes less as the distance becomes greater, then suddenly the person escapes the pull entirely. Muldoon calls this the range of cord-activity. Once the person has managed to get about 10 feet (3 m) away from his or her physical body, he or she is out of cord-activity range and free to go where he or she pleases.

Muldoon says that many people have struggled against the pull of the astral cord without realizing what was happening. Certainly many of us have dreamed of being rooted or frozen in one spot. No matter how hard we struggled, we couldn't break free. We were literally frozen in our tracks.

According to Muldoon, this is the first stage of an astral projection. When it happens, we are already outside our body. Those of us who manage to get beyond cord-activity range may float off anywhere. Those who don't overcome the pull of the astral cord are drawn back into the physical body. Chances are, though, that in either case the experience would be forgotten by the time we got up in the morning.

There is no record of the astral cord ever having been severed during an out-of-the-body experience. The cord is indestructible, Greenhouse tells us, and is severed from the physical body only at death.

And death, says Muldoon, is nothing more or less than a permanent astral projection. As such, it is not something to be feared.

8. THE COMPOSITION AND DRESS OF THE ASTRAL BODY

People undergoing out-of-the-body experiences are usually so confused or thrilled by their new surroundings that they completely ignore the appearance of their spiritual body. Most say that they simply hadn't given it a thought. Some believed that their spiritual body was shapeless and could only compare it to a puff of smoke or a wisp of fog. Some thought that their spiritual body resembled their physical body, and both Muldoon and Carrington insist that this is the case. The astral body is the *exact* duplicate of the physical body, they declare emphatically.

By exact duplicate they are, of course, referring to the shape only. It would be ridiculous to suppose that both bodies were composed of the same substance. The composition of the physical body is well known. The composition of the spiritual body remains a mystery.

This is really not surprising. Although we live with ourselves for a lifetime, we would have great difficulty in describing our physical body. We would probably say that we are made up of flesh, blood, bones, and such things. That would all be true, but it certainly wouldn't be an adequate description.

Students of the occult are naturally eager to identify the substance which makes up the spiritual form. Some believe that it is a substance similar to matter, but with the atoms arranged differently. Others think that it is basically electrical in nature and may be composed of white light. Hereward Carrington frankly admits that he couldn't even make an intelligent guess as to the second body's composition.

The white light theory is perhaps the most interesting one. Muldoon says that an aura of light surrounds the astral cord. There are many reports by people who have seen astral projectors and said that they were bathed in a bright white light. "My daughter came to me after midnight and the brilliance of her image seemed to fill the room," a businessman told Celia Green. "An intensely brilliant bluish-white light suddenly appeared at the foot of my bed," another witness reported. "I was terribly frightened until I recognized my bridge partner standing in the middle of the pool of white light. I wanted to ask her how she had gotten into my bedroom, but she disappeared as suddenly as she came and the room was again in total darkness."

People who have had out-of-the-body experiences are sometimes asked what they wore while in the astral state. This is usually a difficult question to answer. Many people could not describe their astral body, so it would be virtually impossible to tell anyone what they were wearing at the time.

Robert Monroe often projects during the daytime and usually sees himself wearing the same clothes as his physical self had been wearing. On various occasions, he has projected to friends who later gave him an exact description of his suit, shirt, and tie. Monroe is certain, though, that his clothes have no substance. He believes that they are created by thought, but admits that he has no idea how.

Clothing worn in the astral state may sometimes be totally unfamiliar to the projector. Monroe says that he has occasionally had an out-of-the-body experience while wearing a suit and found himself wearing a long, gauzy white robe over his spiritual body. "It was the sort of thing I would never even consider having in the house," he declared.

The long gauzy white robe appears to be the dress of numerous astral projectors. Naturally, this can create certain problems. Ghosts are invariably identified with garments of that description and it's not at all unusual for someone to be mistaken for a ghost while out of his or her body. The astral projector actually is a ghost when seen by others, of course, but his or her physical body is still alive.

A Florida housewife who had had many out-of-the-body experiences described an astral journey to her ex-husband in New York. Although she was with him for only an instant, he carefully noted everything about her appearance. She looked younger, he told her over the phone, her blond hair was much longer, and she was wearing a sleeveless one-piece dress cut low at the neck and reaching almost to her ankles.

The woman was thoroughly confused. Her hair was short and she hadn't worn a dress of that description for ages. Then the pieces began to fall into place.

Her former husband was describing her as she had been when they first met at the house of a friend eighteen years earlier. That was the way she wanted him to remember her and that was how she had appeared before him in her second body. In this case, it seems that desire had formed her astral clothing and youthful appearance.

A Chicago woman told Herbert Greenhouse a similar story. She and her husband, a retired Air Force Colonel, had been married for nearly forty years. Both of them had had frequent out-of-the-body experiences. He was away from home much of the time, but they often visited one another in the second body. She was nearly always able to see him and he could almost always see her. Their manner of dress seldom varied. The husband usually wore the uniform of a young Air Force officer. The wife was usually dressed in the frilly nightdress she had worn as a young bride.

Caroline Larsen, veteran of hundreds of astral journeys and author of *My Travels in the Spirit World,* says, "Spirits, like humans, wear clothes. From every spirit comes a strong light which is completely controlled by the mind. Out of this substance is molded the clothes of the body.

"At first, the molding is in most cases an unconscious act. For no sooner is the spiritual body separated from the physical body than it is in some manner dressed, even though the garment be only a sort of white shroud. But as the mind gains control of itself, the act of dressing becomes a conscious act, and the fashion of the wearing apparel is largely governed by the individual's taste."

51   THE COMPOSITION AND DRESS OF THE ASTRAL BODY

This means, then, that experienced astral projectors can wear whatever they like while in the astral state. All they have to do is to think of what they would like to wear and that's the way they will be dressed.

It's quite possible, too, that they will be able to make themselves appear younger and more attractive.

9 ASTRAL PROJECTIONS DURING TIMES OF ILLNESS

People who are suffering great pain sometimes have an out-of-the-body experience. This seems to be nature's way of easing the agony. Patients have spontaneous projections which grant them at least temporary relief. They might see their tortured body lying on the bed, but they have a peculiar feeling of detachment. Although the person knows that it is his or her body, the person has very little interest in it.

It is not unusual for very sick people who have projected to mention their lack of interest in their physical body. In some cases, the spiritual body actually appears to reject the sick and suffering one. "I know perfectly well that it was me lying there," a woman reported to Crookall, "but I just didn't care. I was happy where I was and I don't think I even felt sorry for the other me. I was only interested in the me that was looking down at myself and I couldn't have cared less about anyone else."

A young mother from Texas reported a rather different type of out-of-the-body experience to Hereward Carrington. She suddenly became terribly ill. The pain was so dreadful that she had to bite her lips to keep from screaming. Her husband rushed her to the hospital, but the pain only grew worse.

Although the doctors did everything in their power, they simply could not discover the source of her problem. As far as the tests were concerned, the woman appeared to be in excellent health. Yet it was obvious to them that she was very sick indeed. She was suffering greatly and growing weaker all the time.

On her third night in the hospital, the woman felt her body become progressively more rigid. She began to shake violently, but she had no control at all over any of her muscles. A bell was within easy reach, but she couldn't ring it to call a nurse. Her muscles simply refused to respond to her will. *That's funny,* she remembered thinking. *I'm not even dead yet and rigor mortis has set in already.*

The next thing the young mother felt was a floating sensation. This was accompanied by a feeling of great happiness. The pain had disappeared entirely and she realized that she had entered a new world. The body lying on the bed belonged to the old world and she had no interest in it.

The new world was delightful. She had never known such happiness and she had never felt better. There was only one problem: She could probably remain there if she wanted to, but she worried that it might not be fair to her husband and two small sons. They loved her very much and they needed her. She also loved them and she would miss them terribly if she stayed in the new world she had entered. If it weren't for her husband and children, though, she would gladly have stayed forever.

ASTRAL PROJECTIONS DURING TIMES OF ILLNESS

Suddenly, she found herself in her own living room. Her husband was reading the Bible and smoking a cigarette. A large ashtray was nearly full of cigarette butts. *Oh, the poor darling,* she said to herself. *This is the first time I've seen him read the Bible and he hasn't smoked a cigarette since he gave up smoking two years ago. He must be worried about me.*

She then floated by the stairs to the room where her four- and six-year-old sons were sleeping. The young mother looked down at them and knew that she would have to return to the body she had left behind in the hospital. She was happy in her new world, but she couldn't stay. Her earthly duties were not yet finished.

She was still looking at her sons when the four-year-old sat straight up in bed. "Mommy!" he called out. "Is that you, Mommy?"

The woman was instantly back in her body and wide awake. She had never heard of an out-of-the-body experience, but she was certain that she had experienced something out of the ordinary. It was not a dream. She was sure of that. She could not, however, imagine how she had suddenly found herself at home.

The fact that she had actually floated home in her second body was confirmed by her husband the next morning. Since her illness, he had been so worried that he had again begun to smoke. He had also tried to find comfort by reading the Bible. He also confirmed the fact that their four-year-old son had called out to her during the night. The little fellow insisted that he had seen his mother dressed in a shiny nightgown and he wanted to kiss her good night.

When a patient is being prepared for an operation, he or she is normally given a gas which produces a state of deep unconsciousness. There are quite a number of cases on record, though, where a patient has had an out-of-the-body experience while under the influence of a drug. The patient usually remained in the operating room and watched everything that went on with great interest. On regaining consciousness, the patient was able to describe the operation and repeat the conversations of the doctors and nurses.

Myrtle Hendry, formerly a nurse in a Chicago hospital, actually saw a patient's second body leave his physical body. It floated up from the operating table and stopped just below the ceiling. It then floated to the floor and stood beside the doctor. While the surgeon performed his delicate task, the patient's astral body stood beside him and carefully observed everything that was going on. The patient later told Nurse Hendry that he had been completely conscious throughout the entire course of the operation.

Dr. J. B. Hout, a retired surgeon, described a similar experience. He was an intern at the time and was in the operating room only as an observer. The patient had barely begun to inhale the gas when Dr. Hout saw a shining form rise from the body on the operating table. It rose slowly to the ceiling trailing what he described as a silvery curl of smoke behind it. (This was obviously the astral cord, but Dr. Hout had never heard of astral projection at that time.)

None of the nurses or any of the other doctors saw anything unusual. Dr. Hout was the only one who saw the astral body and he was reluctant to mention it. He was still an intern and he didn't want anyone to think that he was imagining things. Doctors, he knew, had to be practical and realistic men. He didn't even mention the incident after the patient had described the experience to him in minute detail.

In his book *A Surgeon Remembers,* Dr. George Sava tells about an out-of-the-body experience that made a deep and a lasting impression on him. A patient, Mrs. Francis Gail, had to have a particularly difficult operation. Certain complications arose and the surgeon discussed the problem with the doctors who were assisting him. "Do you think she can stand it?" one asked when they had decided what measures they would now have to take. "I hope so," Dr. Sava replied, then added, "She seems to be a pretty tough old bird."

Shortly after regaining consciousness, Mrs. Gail told Dr. Sava a story that astounded him. She had left her body immediately after being given the gas and had entered a place of love and happiness. She decided not to stay there, however, because her family still needed her. Once that decision had been made, her second body returned to the hospital.

Mrs. Gail was a keen observer. She described accurately the discussion that had taken place among the doctors. She knew that there had been complications and that the doctors were worried about her ability to stand the operation. "But you said that I seemed to be a pretty tough old bird, didn't you, Dr. Sava?" she asked with a smile.

Dr. Sava didn't know what to think. The patient had been given a drug. She should have been in a state of deep unconsciousness, yet she had been aware of everything that was taking place. While the doctors were operating on her physical body, she was watching the entire procedure from her spiritual body.

The patient's account of her out-of-the-body experience rather disturbed the surgeon. "I found it difficult to accept the thought that when I operated, the patient's astral body might be hovering overhead carefully observing my every move," he wrote, adding, "I must admit, however, that this appears to be a fascinating but frightening possibility."

This might explain, too, why some doctors are reluctant to accept the theory of astral projection.

10 ASTRAL PROJECTIONS AT THE TIME OF AN ACCIDENT

In 1974, a group of men met in the suite of a hotel in Los Angeles. The group included psychologists, psychiatrists, parapsychologists, and doctors. There were also nine people present who claimed that they were able to leave their physical bodies behind and travel in their spiritual bodies. The purpose of the meeting was to discuss the unsolved mysteries of astral projection.

Several of the men insisted that astral projection was nothing more than a vivid dream. A California doctor, however, made a brave effort to illustrate the difference between a dream and an out-of-the-body experience. Some years earlier, he had been in a serious accident while on his way to an emergency call. He was hurled from his car and landed unconscious on the highway. Then, to his astonishment, the doctor found himself floating about 8 feet (2.44 m) above his physical body. Every faculty was perfectly alert. He heard the scream of sirens and watched with interest as his unconscious form was carried into an ambulance. Still floating in the air, the doctor observed everything that took place in the emergency ward of the hospital. He did not reenter his physical body until he had been wheeled into a private room.

ASTRAL PROJECTIONS AT THE TIME OF AN ACCIDENT

"But how do you know that you didn't just dream all this?" someone asked. "How can you prove that this actually happened?"

"I *can't* prove it," the doctor admitted frankly. "I am fully convinced in my own mind, though, that a second body was floating above my physical body. This second body was conscious and completely aware of everything that was going on. I can't prove it, of course," he repeated, a smile on his face, "but I know very well that all this was not a dream. It was something I actually experienced."

Those in the group who had made a serious study of astral projection had no reason to doubt the doctor's story. They all knew that the spiritual body sometimes leaves the natural body when there is a threat of sudden death or painful injury. In such cases, the projection is always instantaneous.

This does not mean, though, that the physical body escapes harm. Far from it. The accident still happens and the victim may be seriously injured. The victim escapes pain and shock only until the two bodies are joined together again.

Hughie Green, a British television star, described an out-of-the-body experience to Celia Green, Director of Britain's Institute of Psychophysical Research. He was involved in a car accident, but left his body a fraction of a second before the impact. Although he could see that he was badly hurt, he was strangely unconcerned. He was more interested in watching the people rushing to the scene than he was in his other self. When the ambulance arrived, he stood at the edge of the crowd and watched the drivers pull his physical body from the wreckage. "I knew it was me," he told Miss Green, "but I just wasn't interested."

A woman who had been hit by a car sent the following brief report to Celia Green at the University of Oxford:

> I was knocked down when the car hit me, but I got to my feet right away. I was surprised that I didn't feel any pain or see any bruises. I seemed to be all right, so I started walking home. I saw people running from all directions and I looked around to see what was happening.
>
> Then I saw that my body was still lying in the street and they were running toward that. Some of the people ran right through me as I stood there. This seemed rather strange and I walked back to my body. I thought I was my normal self because my new body behaved exactly like the one that had been hit by the car. When I got close to the body that had been hit, I had the feeling that I was being pulled back inside.
>
> I didn't remember anything more until I regained consciousness in the hospital.

This was the woman's one and only out-of-the-body experience. She apparently went into shock when the car hit her and she immediately left her body. She didn't feel any pain after her projection although she knew that she had been knocked down by a car. Everything seemed normal to her until she looked back and saw herself lying in the street. As soon as she got close to her physical body, she was immediately drawn back into it.

In another case, an accident victim tried to help his physical body while astrally projected. A young man lost control of his motorcycle while riding at high speed on a busy highway. Terror seized him, then suddenly subsided. He was now standing calmly in the middle of the road in another body. His natural body lay unconscious beside the curb with the motorcycle on top of it.

Although he was only mildly curious, the young man strolled over to have a look at himself. Blood was spurting from a deep cut on his forehead and another on his cheek. One leg was badly twisted and was most likely broken. *The poor devil really got himself banged up,* he thought.

Two men came hurrying over and took quick action. "Let's get that motorcycle off him!" one exclaimed. The young man stepped forward to help them. There was nothing he could do, however. When he bent down to assist the two men, he was pulled back into his physical body. His projection had lasted only a matter of a few seconds, but it was an experience he would never forget.

In *The Astral Journey*, Greenhouse tells about a man named Roger Oppermann who was in the astral state for more than five hours. The man was thrown from his horse and knocked unconscious. When he finally regained consciousness, he was able to describe accurately everything that had happened.

Two farmers had witnessed the accident and carried the man to a nearby house. A doctor was called, but he feared a skull fracture and said that the patient had to be taken to the hospital. Over three more hours passed before the injured man opened his eyes and looked around him.

To the doctor's complete surprise, the patient remembered every detail of the afternoon. He described the men who had picked him up and he described the people in the farmhouse. The ambulance driver had red hair, he said, and his assistant had a bushy mustache. The patient was even able to repeat much of the conversation that had taken place.

"But how do you know all this?" asked the astonished doctor. "You were completely unconscious all that time."

"No, you're wrong, Doctor," the injured man replied. "I have never in all my life been as conscious as I was this afternoon. I was in a beautiful world that I very much want to see again and I know that I will."

11 A DOCTOR'S STORY

Dr. Raymond Moody, author of *Life After Life,* prefers the term *near-death experience* to out-of-the-body experience. This is quite understandable. Being a doctor, he is often in contact with people who are seriously ill or have been seriously injured. Some of these people told him about unusual experiences they had undergone during their illnesses and they all seemed to have been deeply moved by them.

In the beginning, Dr. Moody did not take his patients' stories too seriously. They were very sick people and may very well have been imagining things. The stories interested him, however, and he mentioned some of them to the nurses and other doctors in the hospital. To his surprise, he learned that they had all heard virtually the same accounts from other patients. It was then that Dr. Moody began his study of what he called near-death experiences.

During the course of his study, Dr. Moody discovered a striking resemblance among the accounts of the experiences themselves. Although none of the descriptions were exactly identical, all of them had several points in common. There was not in any case any reason to doubt the complete sincerity of the patient.

The patients usually began their stories by saying that they had suddenly found themselves outside of their physical body. This was a brand new experience to them and they didn't quite know what to think of it. They were confused and perhaps even a bit frightened. Their own body was still lying on the hospital bed, but it seemed strange and unfamiliar.

Dr. Moody soon learned that the patients found it very difficult to describe their second body. Many said that they were so interested in the new world they had entered that they simply never gave their body a thought. Others were certain that their second body was weightless. "I couldn't have weighed anything," said one patient, "because I floated right up to the ceiling and then up and down the corridors in the hospital."

Muldoon and Carrington insist that the spiritual body is the exact duplicate of the physical body. Patients who have studied themselves while in the astral state tend to agree. "Oh, it was me all right," a woman declared. "I looked just like myself, but I didn't feel any pain or anything and I could float all over the place. It was really lovely and I felt so sorry when I had to go back to that old, sick body of mine."

A reluctance to return to the physical body was reported frequently. The initial feeling of fear was very quickly replaced by a feeling of great peace. The sick and injured were free from pain and free to go wherever they wished. Once they became accustomed to their second body, they found it vastly superior in every respect. It was only those with close family ties who felt no regret when they were drawn back into their physical selves.

People who had left their bodies told Dr. Moody that they had been able to see and hear much more clearly while in the astral state. "It seemed as though I was able to see everything there was to see in the whole world," one reported. "My vision was actually limitless. I could see through hills and over the oceans." "I just couldn't understand how I could see so far," another declared. An elderly woman insisted that she had 360 degree vision while in her second body, but her physical self could see almost nothing without glasses.

Hearing appears to be a very different thing entirely. Most said that they did not actually hear any voices or sounds. They just seemed to pick up the thoughts of those around them. There was no need for words because they knew what a person was going to say before a word was even spoken. Nobody, however, ever complained about the silence of the astral world.

A number of patients who had undergone near-death experiences told Dr. Moody that they had been projected toward a distant light. As they came closer, the light became brighter and brighter. It was brighter than anything they could have imagined, but it didn't dazzle or hurt their eyes. In spite of the unearthly brilliance, they were still able to see everything clearly.

"A Being of Light" is Dr. Moody's term for what his patients have seen and few doubted that the light was actually a personal being. The personal being, most believed, had to be God. Love and warmth poured forth from Him and the astral projector was happy and serene in His presence. It was invariably a far greater happiness than ever before experienced. "For the first time in my life, I had complete peace of mind and a sense of joy which I cannot even begin to describe," a man in his early fifties told Dr. Moody.

Astral projectors who claim to have seen God also tell strikingly similar stories about their conversations with Him. Although a few say that they heard His voice, the rest of them say that they heard nothing. Conversation took place by transfer of thought only. Each understood the other perfectly and no words were needed.

This is precisely what happens when someone meets a dead relative or friend while in the second body. There is instant communication, and there is no need for words. This is fortunate because the second body has no voice. It can hear, but it cannot be heard.

People had trouble explaining just how they told God what they had done with their lives. "I just thought about it and He read my mind," declared one woman. "I didn't have to say a word." "It just happened," said another woman, "and it must have happened at the speed of light. Everything I had ever said or done from the time I was a baby was right there in front of me. There was so much that I thought I had forgotten, but it was all there and it all came rushing back when I saw it."

Those who have had out-of-the-body experiences are often reluctant to discuss them with other people. Those who say that they have seen God during a near-death experience are understandably even more reluctant to tell anyone about it. Nobody likes to be looked upon as a crackpot, so these people usually keep their stories to themselves. This makes the job of the researcher much more difficult, but we can hardly blame anyone for that. And it's true, of course, that we're all apt to look rather strangely upon anyone who says that they've seen God.

Over the years, Dr. Moody has talked to nearly 200 people who have had out-of-the-body experiences. He is absolutely convinced that these people are telling the truth. "Their near-death experiences were very real events to these people, and through my association with them the experiences have become real events to me," he declares.

It is not possible for Dr. Moody to draw any conclusions based on his investigations. He readily admits that the constitution of the spiritual body is a complete mystery to him. Neither does he pretend to know why some patients have near-death experiences and others do not. His findings cannot be analyzed in a laboratory because he has no hard, cold, scientific facts to work with. "I am fully aware that my work on near-death experiences does not constitute a scientific study," he says. "We must, however, have the courage to open new doors and admit that our present-day scientific tools are not adequate for many of these new investigations."

Fortunately, there are more and more serious investigators who are willing to study a subject which has still not been accepted as a scientific fact. This may not help their professional reputations, but it may help us to understand ourselves.

12 LIFE AFTER DEATH

There are many doctors who have had patients come back from the dead. This does not mean that the person had died and been buried. It means that the person had been pronounced clinically dead by the doctor, then came back to life a few minutes later.

Dr. Elisabeth Kubler-Ross, author of *The Experience of Dying,* is perhaps America's foremost authority on people who have come back from the dead. During her medical career, she has interviewed hundreds of people revived from clinical death. Her research has convinced her that there is something about the death experience which removes the person's fear of dying.

Dr. Kubler-Ross has been quoted as saying, "I'm totally convinced that there is life after death. I've seen more than 1,000 people die—and before they died all of them left strong evidence of life after death."

Dr. Karlis Osis of the American Society for Psychical Research agrees. "I believe in life after death," he says. "I also believe that the only way for there to be an existence after death is for the spiritual body to leave the physical body and travel to another reality.

Out-of-the-body experiences are the only way for this departure of the spiritual body to occur."

Sylvan Muldoon said essentially the same thing. "Death," he declared, "is merely a permanent astral projection." If that is true, then temporary death is merely a temporary astral projection.

A sick person who has come back from the dead and a healthy person who has had an out-of-the-body experience frequently tell strikingly similar stories. The first feeling is often a floating sensation. A man finds himself suspended near the ceiling and sees his physical body lying in bed. If there are other people in the room, he can see them and hear them. There is no way, though, in which he can communicate with anyone else. Normally, the second body can be neither seen nor heard and this often brings on a feeling of great loneliness.

The spiritual body then moves—at the speed of thought as it were—into a warm and wonderful new world. Spirits of dead friends and relatives come to greet the body and the loneliness disappears. Many also see a being of light which is often described as God. This being of light asks the spiritual body what he or she has done with his or her life on earth and the entire story pours forth spontaneously.

It can easily be understood why people who have entered this wonderful world are reluctant to leave it. They are entirely free of pain or worry. They are surrounded by love and feel a happiness which they have never before experienced. But they cannot stay. They are not yet ready for the new world they have entered, and a force which cannot be resisted pulls them back into their physical self.

Only a very few of the hundreds of people interviewed by Dr. Kubler-Ross were frightened by the thought of death. When their time came to die, they felt strangely unafraid. Something they couldn't explain told them that death was a joyous experience which need not be feared. One woman remembers thinking, "Oh, I'm dead! How lovely!"

Another said, "I knew I was dead and I wasn't sorry, but I just couldn't figure out what I was supposed to do. I kept thinking, *My God, I'm dead! I can't believe it!* I never really believed, you see, that I was going to die. Death was always something that happened to the other person, but I just never thought it would happen to me. I'm glad it did, though, because now I know that death is a wonderful experience."

A college student who came back from the dead told Dr. Kubler-Ross, "I didn't want to come back. Death is nice. It was the loveliest thing that ever happened to me. I appreciate life more now, but I'm not scared of dying."

"I was so happy being dead," another young patient declared.

A businessman who "died" of a heart attack and lived to tell about it said, "The death experience is beautiful. I really enjoyed it. I even struggled against being brought back to this life. The experience is something I'd like to feel again. It completely changed the way I see myself and those around me. It changed my life for the better."

The great majority of people who came back from the dead said that they were now living richer and fuller lives. They found more pleasure in the simple things and were more considerate of others. Life was something to be enjoyed. Each day was to be lived to the fullest. Many who had often been depressed and bored before their death experience immediately adopted a wholesome and happy attitude toward life.

Strangely enough, only a very few people said that their experience with death had made them more religious. Those who had attended church regularly continued to do so. Those who had not attended church did not suddenly become Sunday School teachers. Their experience was an intensely private one and they didn't care to share it with the world. "How could I possibly tell anyone that I went to Heaven and talked with God?" asked one patient, adding, "My friends would think that I was out of my mind."

This is undoubtedly true. People were reluctant to discuss their experience with others because they feared ridicule. Most of those who told their doctor what had happened to them while they were dead asked that their names not be used in any publication.

There was one man, however, who felt that his story had to be told. His name is Victor Solow and his story appeared in the *Reader's Digest*. The title of the article was "I Died at 10:52 A.M."

"It was a very private moment, but I wanted to write about it so that others would know that death is not something to be feared," he told David Wheeler, author of *Journey to the Other Side*. "I had no intention, though, of attempting to convince others of my experience. In fact, I do not really care if they believe me. I *know* what happened, but there is no way that I can make others share my experience or make them believe my story. I can only say that before I died, I was always pretty tense and unhappy with the world. After experiencing death, my relationship with this life has become much more meaningful."

Others who "died" and lived to tell about it have felt very much the same way.

13 DO-IT-YOURSELF ASTRAL PROJECTION

Temporary death is a temporary astral projection. We do not have to be pronounced dead, of course, to have an out-of-the-body experience. There are several books on the market which give the reader step-by-step directions for leaving the body. Unfortunately, the directions are very difficult to follow and there is no way of knowing how many people were actually able to leave their body after studying one of these books. Chances are, though, that the success rate is very small indeed.

Robert Monroe, Director of the Monroe Institute of Applied Sciences in Afton, Virginia, has probably taught more people how to have conscious out-of-the-body experiences than anyone else. He teaches astral projection on weekends and estimates that he has taught several hundred people how to leave their bodies. Although Monroe did not have an out-of-the-body experience until he was an adult, he has been having them regularly since.

Monroe believes that just about anyone can leave the physical body behind and travel in the astral world if the desire is great enough. He or she may not succeed on every attempt, but most people should have at least as many successes as failures. Those who fail repeatedly are those who have failed to overcome certain barriers.

The greatest barrier of all is fear. An astral journey is a journey into the unknown. Nobody is really sure what to expect there and everyone is somewhat nervous and apprehensive. It's not always easy to overcome our fears when we're in familiar territory. It's much more difficult, then, to be calm and unafraid when we're about to enter a different world.

Nearly every writer on the techniques of astral projection stresses the fact that total relaxation is of the utmost importance. This, of course, presents a problem. A person cannot be relaxed if he or she is worried or afraid. People must overcome all their fears before they can hope to relax. Until that is accomplished, a conscious projection is virtually impossible.

Complete relaxation presents problems of its own. It's much easier to relax in bed than anywhere else. The trouble is, people are usually tired when they go to bed. If they attempt a conscious projection at that time, chances are they will fall asleep as soon as they are sufficiently relaxed. One astral projector admitted that it took him twelve years to achieve a conscious projection because he always kept falling asleep.

The above is an extreme case, of course, but a conscious projection does take a lot of practice. Monroe says that people shouldn't be discouraged if they fail on their first attempts. If they fall asleep, it's nothing to worry about. One can always try again the next night. With effort and patience, one should in time be able to reach a state of total relaxation. After the first success, the following attempts become easier and easier.

Robert Moser, author of *Mental and Astral Projection,* believes that the secret of relaxation is correct breathing. By deep and rhythmic breathing, people soon reach a point where they are hovering between being awake and being asleep. At this point, they must struggle to maintain consciousness.

The best way to maintain consciousness is to concentrate on the place you want to visit. Moser insists that this is vitally important. Unless you have a destination in mind, your astral journey is apt to take you just about anywhere. Many people have found themselves in places they had no desire to see or with people who were strangers to them, Moser tells us.

Both Muldoon and Carrington are of the opinion that an experienced astral projector can almost always go exactly where he or she wants to go. They admit, though, that the spiritual body sometimes has a mind of its own. It goes where it wants to go and nothing can be done about it.

Then, too, there are times when even the most experienced astral projector simply cannot get out of his or her physical body. Although one may have had hundreds of out-of-the-body experiences, he or she will suddenly be unable to project. If that happens to professional projectors, the amateur shouldn't be too discouraged by these initial failures.

According to a full-page advertisement in a recent issue of *Fate* magazine, out-of-the-body experiences can be automatically triggered by certain sounds. The advertisement says:

Recent experiments prove that out-of-the-body experiences can be induced by simply listening to certain sounds which can automatically stimulate a pleasure center in your mind while it creates a warm, comfortable vibration throughout the body. These sounds, known as "Astral Sounds" have triggered out-of-the-body experiences in persons who have tried other methods that have failed.

Users say these "Astral Sounds" create physical sensations of such intense pleasure that many people could not find words to describe the feeling.

And it's all so easy to do. Just relax, switch on your tape cassette of "Astral Sounds" and let your mind and body enjoy them. The incredible sounds on the tape can automatically carry you into an unforgettable world of pure pleasure! Send for yours today!

The tape cassette of "Astral Sounds" costs only a few dollars. It's cheap if it works, but you don't get your money back if it doesn't.

14 DANGERS OF ASTRAL PROJECTION

Can a conscious astral projection prove harmful to the person journeying outside the body? This is a perfectly valid question, but most writers choose to ignore it. Oliver Fox is the only one who discusses it at any length. He confesses, though, that he is not on very firm ground. Although he has never faced any dangers himself, he thinks that some may possibly exist.

This was most likely a gentle warning to anyone planning to have a conscious out-of-the-body experience. Fox did most of his astral wandering in the early 1900s. He was one of the first Westerners to study the phenomenon in depth. Much of astral projection is still a mystery, but it was much more of a mystery seventy-five years ago. There was almost no information available on the subject at that time and Fox had no way of knowing whether the practice was dangerous or not.

It was Fox's belief that astral projection should not be practiced by very excitable and nervous people. They may lack self-control and the experience might prove to be too much of a strain on them. The shock of leaving the body, he says, might cause a nervous disorder or a heart attack. No one with a weak heart or a nervous condition should ever attempt a conscious projection, he wrote.

Fox stressed the fact that he was giving his opinion and his opinion only. There was no scientific basis for anything he wrote. Astral projection was virtually unheard of at the beginning of this century and Fox was covering new ground. We can hardly blame him for warning people of dangers which he honestly thought might exist.

Dr. Robert Crookall also gives his readers a gentle warning in *The Study and Practice of Astral Projection.* He tells us that an out-of-the-body experience should never be forced in any way. If it happens naturally, that's all well and good. A forced projection, on the other hand, could cause damage to the projector. We are not told, however, what form this damage might take.

Herbert Greenhouse also leaves the reader pretty much in the dark. He tells us all about the joys of astral travel. We're told about the glories of the astral world and the happiness we'll find there. The astral cord is normally indestructible, he says, and is severed from the physical body only at the time of death. We don't have to worry, though, about this happening accidentally during an out-of-the-body experience.

Astral projection, he then says, is not recommended for amateurs. No one should even consider attempting an out-of-the-body experience unless they have first consulted a parapsychologist or a person who has done a great deal of astral projection. And above all, he warns in big, bold letters, DO NOT SUBSCRIBE TO MAIL-ORDER COURSES IN ASTRAL PROJECTION.

A rather interesting and unusual danger is described by Robert Moser. The astral world is so beautiful and exciting, he claims, that the astral projector faces the danger of staying there too long. The lure of the unknown keeps getting stronger, but the temptation to remain must be resisted. If it is not resisted, it may become so strong that it can easily grow out of control. The astral projector will then lose all desire to return to the physical body.

It seems that Moser differs from other writers on this point. Many people said that they were reluctant to return to their physical body. They wanted to stay where they were. Although many struggled to stay in the astral world, they were pulled irresistibly back into themselves. They had absolutely no choice in the matter. The decision to return was made for them.

Then, too, time is an unknown dimension in the astral world. People never know how long their dreams last. Neither do they know how long they have been out of their physical body. Hours may seem like seconds or seconds may seem like hours. If they have no sense of time, they will have no way of knowing whether or not they are staying away for too long. This is probably one reason why the return to the physical self seems to be triggered automatically. A projector is returned to the physical body when it's time to return.

Muldoon and Carrington have written the most comprehensive books on astral projection and neither of them say that a conscious projection can be a dangerous practice. They simply say that not every out-of-the-body experience is a pleasant one. An unpleasant astral journey, however, is no more dangerous than a bad dream.

In *The Projection of the Astral Body* Muldoon stresses the fact that a person should never attempt a conscious projection when in the wrong state of mind. This would not be dangerous, but it might be unpleasant. It would also be very foolish. If a person is depressed or unhappy on leaving the physical body, he or she will most likely be exactly the same way in the spiritual body. In such a case, an astral projection could hardly be a happy experience.

In one rather weird experiment, Muldoon proved to his own satisfaction that the second body cannot be harmed in any way. He placed thirty needles, points downward, in a board, then fastened the board to the head and foot of his bed. When he was lying flat on his back, the needle-embedded board was approximately 18 inches (46 cm) above him.

During the course of the next week, he had several conscious projections. On two occasions, he was totally aware of the fact that his second body was passing through the board. Although he could see the needles, he felt absolutely nothing at all. As a result of that experiment, he concluded that the spiritual self could not be harmed and could not feel pain.

The same conclusion has been reached by Robert Monroe. He has taught the techniques of conscious astral projection to hundreds of people and not a single one has faced danger in any form. A few were

85 DANGERS OF ASTRAL PROJECTION

frightened by their first glimpse of the unknown, but that fear soon passed.

"Physical life," says Monroe, "is much more dangerous than the spiritual life. We face dangers daily here on earth, but we cannot be harmed while in the astral world. Our spiritual body is indestructible."

15 CHILDREN'S OUT-OF-THE-BODY EXPERIENCES

Children, too, have out-of-the-body experiences, but they are almost always spontaneous. They are accepted as something that just happens, so there is very seldom any attempt at conscious projection. It would simply never occur to a child to try to leave his or her physical body behind and float around in the second body.

A strange case of childhood projection is described by Herbert Greenhouse in *The Astral Journey*. Carol White, a nine-year-old schoolgirl, left her physical body practically every night. Although she seldom left her bedroom, she did on rare occasions find herself in unfamiliar places. This didn't worry her in the least. Her real body, as she called it, was still in bed and she knew that it was safe there.

Then one night a disturbing thought crossed Carol's mind. "What would happen, Mommy," she asked, "if somebody kidnapped my real body while I was somewhere else? Would I die?"

Mrs. White gave her daughter a puzzled look. She didn't have the faintest idea what the girl was talking about. She still didn't quite know what to think when

Carol said that she had been leaving her real body on the bed for years and floating around in another body.

It surprised Carol to learn that her experience was a rather unusual one. Up until that time, she had accepted her out-of-the-body journeys as natural, everyday events. She had not discussed them with her mother or her friends because she thought the same thing happened to everybody.

Greenhouse also describes the experience of a girl called Kathy who lived in New York. Kathy had trouble making friends and spent much of her time alone. She was far more comfortable reading a book in her bedroom than she was in the company of other people.

Kathy's strange behavior worried her parents. She was eleven years old and she didn't have a friend in the world. None of the other girls ever called her on the phone or came to visit her. The other girls walked back and forth to school in happy little groups. Their daughter walked by herself.

The parents finally decided that Kathy should join a girls club. It was just about the last thing on earth that she wanted to do, but her father and mother were insistent. They didn't want their daughter to go through life without having a single friend.

At one of the meetings, the girls began playing a game in the high school gym. Kathy was not invited to join them and she stood on the sidelines watching. She felt terribly left out of things, but she couldn't leave until the meeting was over.

While she was watching, a very strange feeling

came over her. She gave a sudden shudder, then felt herself floating high up to the ceiling of the gymnasium. It was a wonderful sensation and she was completely unafraid. She just wished that the other girls would look up and see her.

A moment or two passed before Kathy saw something which really surprised her. She saw herself standing on the sidelines watching the game. That's funny, she thought. I know that I'm up here, but I can also see myself down there. I wonder how that can be. The situation amused her and she thinks she gave a little laugh.

Kathy told Greenhouse that she was out of her body for about half an hour. She watched the girls playing their game and she also watched herself. When the game ended, she descended slowly and merged easily with her physical body. She no longer felt inferior or left out. She had floated through the air and she was sure none of the other girls had ever done that.

It was most likely loneliness that brought on Kathy's out-of-the-body experience. In a case mentioned by both Greenhouse and Crookall, the experience was brought on by fear and stress. A five-year-old boy suddenly left his body after he had fallen into a river and was in danger of drowning. His terror disappeared and he entered a world of great peace and beauty.

The boy was very happy in the new world he had entered. It was a warm and wonderful place filled with soothing music. Dead relatives that he recognized from the family album were there. Much more impor-

CHILDREN'S OUT-OF-THE-BODY EXPERIENCES

tant, his mother who had died the year before was also there and she was even more beautiful than he remembered her. She bent down to kiss him and a black cross with seven sparkling stars on it slipped out of her blouse. He reached out for the cross, but he was unable to touch it. His mother suddenly jerked away from him. She became smaller and smaller until she disappeared in the distance. At the exact moment of her disappearance, the boy regained consciousness. His brothers had pulled him out of the river and had managed to revive him.

That evening, the boy told his father what he had seen while unconscious. When he said that his mother had been wearing a black cross with seven sparkling stars on it, the father gasped in astonishment. He had once bought just such a cross as a birthday present for his wife. Unfortunately, she had died three days before her birthday. While she was in the coffin, he had slipped the cross into her folded hands. His son could not possibly have seen the cross at that time because he had been sent to the home of an aunt when his mother died.

There could be only one explanation: The boy had actually seen his mother while visiting another world and she had been wearing the black cross with the seven sparkling stars.

Herbert Greenhouse says that children's out-of-the-body experiences usually begin at the age of four. Ingo Swann, however, was projecting regularly from his home in Colorado before his third birthday.

In *To Kiss Earth Good-Bye,* Swann tells about describing one of his astral journeys to his grandmother. The year was 1936 and a bloody civil war was raging in Spain. He saw people flying in big birds, he said, and they dropped things that made big explosions when they hit the ground. Men were killing other men and everybody else was running away. People were yelling and shouting in a language like the Mexicans spoke, but these people weren't Mexicans.

Although his grandmother suggested that he had been dreaming, Swann insisted otherwise. "I was there," he said. "I floated across a big ocean with huge waves and I saw these things. In a dream, I just stay in one place."

Swann also tells how he shocked a doctor and nurse when he was only three years old. He had to have his tonsils removed and a nurse held an ether mask over his face. As soon as he lost consciousness, his second body floated slowly up to the ceiling. From that vantage point, he watched everything that went on with great interest. He could hear what the doctor and nurse were saying and he heard the doctor swear when he dropped something onto the floor.

When the effects of the sedative wore off, Swann described the operation in detail. He even told the doctor and nurse what had been done with his tonsils. "And you used a naughty word," he told the doctor. "You dropped something onto the floor and then you used a naughty word."

"But how do you know that?" asked the doctor. "The nurse put you to sleep."

"I was up on the ceiling," Swann said matter-of-factly, "and I saw everything and I heard everything."

The doctor and nurse could only shake their heads. Neither of them were familiar with out-of-the-body experiences and they couldn't imagine how the child could have known these things.

16 SOME REASONS FOR CONSCIOUS ASTRAL PROJECTIONS

When Robert Moser asked one of his classes why they wanted to learn the techniques of astral projection, he found that most of the students had perfectly valid reasons. A few said that they wanted to experience the thrills of astral travel. Some wanted to see the strange and beautiful world they had heard about. Others believed that the experience would help them spiritually. And one student said that he wanted to learn astral projection so that he could find out what was going on in the house across the street from his.

The desire to be with someone who you think needs you is a reason often given for conscious projections. Dr. Crookall tells about a man who journeyed from upstate New York to Florida to see a sick friend. The sick friend was a woman he had once loved. He was, in fact, still very fond of her. Something told him that she needed help and he immediately projected to her side.

"An intense desire to see her seized me," he wrote to Crookall. "It seemed to be an impelling force and I flew with incredible speed through the darkness. The lakes and mountains were lost to view almost immediately. Then other lakes and mountains came within view of my astonished vision. But I became so confused while journeying that I hardly noticed the landscape far below me until I came to a certain point on the road. 'She is there' I said under my breath, 'and she is suffering.' "

The woman was all alone in her apartment. She had a book on her lap, but wasn't reading it. Although she looked up for a moment when her astral visitor entered the room, she didn't seem to be aware of anyone's presence.

It was a terribly frustrating time for the man from New York. No matter how hard he tried, he could not get her attention. There was no way in which he could make himself seen or heard or felt.

Then a very strange thing happened! The woman got up from her chair, walked slowly across the room, and stood by her dresser looking at an old photograph of her astral visitor. As soon as she returned to her chair, the man was pulled back into his physical body in New York.

In another case described by Crookall, a British officer stationed in Nigeria in West Africa entered his spiritual body to search for his brother. His brother lived in New Zealand. He usually wrote regularly, but the letters had suddenly stopped coming.

Just seconds after leaving his body, the officer found himself standing in a snow-covered churchyard. He knew at once where he was. The church was in Braemar, Hampshire, in England and his family had attended services there for many years.

Some force now directed the officer to the graveyard behind the church. He already knew, though, what he would find there. There was a new tombstone under a yew tree and his brother's name was on it. The officer learned later that his brother had come home unexpectedly from New Zealand, contracted pneumonia, and died a week later.

Yram, a pseudonym of the author of *Practical Astral Projection,* often left his physical body to partake of the joys of the astral world. When he left his physical body behind, he also left all his earthly cares and worries behind. "In the astral world," he wrote, "the most minute details are extraordinarily clear. The whole of the body is impregnated with a joy which is, at once, so gentle and yet so powerful that tears spring to the eyes. It is impossible to express adequately a state of happiness so complete, so real, and so vivid. Any form of earthly exaltation is a poor analogy, because we have never been so peaceful and calm before."

There was another reason, too, for Yram's frequent astral journeys. A young woman of whom he was very fond moved to a town several hundred miles away. Yram visited her in his second body almost every night and soon fell deeply in love with her. The young lady was never able to see her astral visitor, but she always sensed his presence. Yram tells us that he proposed to the young woman while out of his body and that she accepted his proposal. He then taught her astral projection and they were soon journeying together on the astral plane.

Sylvan Muldoon also married a girl he often visited while out of his body. Oliver Fox, Robert Monroe, and others often projected to the homes of lady friends. Elsie, Fox's fiance, often scolded him for entering her bedroom at night in his spiritual body, but Monroe had a more serious problem. He would sometimes enter the bedrooms of women he hardly knew. Although he was afraid that someone might recognize him, he still found himself in places where he knew he shouldn't be.

Many conscious out-of-the-body experiences are triggered by love. This means more, of course, than Oliver Fox's astral journeys to Elsie. It also means the love of a mother for her child or the love of a man for his wife. Greenhouse says that astral projectors go most often where their affections take them. This refers to spontaneous as well as to conscious projections.

Another compelling reason for conscious out-of-the-body experiences is the thrill of the astral journey itself. Charles Tart, Professor of Psychology at the University of California in Davis, estimates that about 90 or 95 percent of all astral journeys are extremely joyful. Most writers seem to agree. Unpleasant out-of-the-body experiences are certainly not unheard of, but the overwhelming majority are almost unbelievably thrilling and lovely.

It's not surprising, then, that experienced astral projectors often leave their physical bodies behind and zoom off into the astral world in their second bodies.

17 ASTRAL PROJECTION IN THE LABORATORY

"There is as yet no known way to prove that a person has had an out-of-the-body experience," says Robert Monroe. "The scientists just have to take the projector's word as evidence of proof."

But taking someone's word for something is not good enough for the men of science. If it were, astral projection would have been accepted as a scientific fact long ago. There are many case histories of out-of-the-body experiences on record at Duke University, the University of Virginia, Stanford Research Institute, the American Society for Psychical Research, and a number of other institutions. People like Greenhouse, Muldoon, Monroe, Carrington, Crookall, and Celia Green have collected many more. Astral projection is undoubtedly a reality, but it's a terribly difficult thing to prove in a laboratory.

Scientists are, by the very nature of their profession, practical people. They demand proof before they will accept anything as a scientific fact. An out-of-the-body experience cannot be observed or measured, and that complicates the issue.

Most of what is known about out-of-the-body experiences comes from people who have had the experience only once in their lifetime. This puts the scientists at a disadvantage. The experience can be described, but it usually cannot be produced at will. Because it cannot be produced at will, it cannot ordinarily be studied under controlled laboratory conditions.

Another disadvantage is that descriptions of the out-of-the-body experiences are usually lacking in detail. This is not at all surprising. People who suddenly find themselves in another world are apt to be rather poor observers. They are too excited and too busy to study the things they see. It must be remembered, too, that many of the things people have seen on the astral plane would be difficult to describe.

"It would be of great advantage in studying out-of-the-body experiences," declared Charles Tart, "to have trained people available who could produce the experience at will and who generally had the characteristics of a good reporter." Fortunately, Dr. Tart has on occasion had the opportunity to study several such trained travelers. One of them is Robert Monroe, a veteran of hundreds of astral journeys.

The first series of laboratory studies was carried out at the University of Virginia Medical School and took place over a period of eight nights. Monroe was hooked up to various instruments which were to measure his heartbeat, eye movements, and brain waves. A laboratory technician in the next room was supposed to keep a close check on the instrument readings.

It was not until the eighth night that Monroe was

able to enter his spiritual body. He then floated into the adjoining room, but there was nobody there. He next floated out into the corridor. The laboratory technician was there leaning against the wall talking to a man. Monroe was unable to make his presence known and soon slipped back into his physical body.

The lab technician readily confessed to having neglected her duties for a short time. Her husband had stopped by and she had left the room to talk to him. It was during this time that Monroe had projected and seen them together.

Tart's most dramatic experiment was with a young woman he refers to only as Miss Z. Out-of-the-body experiences were so normal for her that she seldom gave them a thought. As far as she could recall, she had been having them all her life. She would wake up at night and find herself floating near the ceiling while her physical body lay quietly in bed. She assumed that this sort of thing happened to everyone. It was not until she was a teenager that she began to realize that her experiences were rather unusual.

Miss Z was glad to work together with Tart. She had never made any attempt to control her projections because the idea had simply never occurred to her. When Tart suggested to her that this might be possible, she became very interested.

The plan sounded simple enough: The psychologist would write five numbers on a slip of paper. This would be placed on a shelf near the ceiling. Miss Z would lie on a cot hooked up to various instruments. If she fell asleep and had an out-of-the-body experience, she was to float up to the ceiling and memorize the number. She was then to wake up immediately and tell Tart what the number was.

Nothing very exciting happened the first three nights. Then, just as Miss Z was due to be awakened after her fourth night's sleep, she awoke and sat up on her cot. "The number," she announced, "is 2-5-1-3-2."

Tart was jubilant. Miss Z had called out the right number. She had not, however, proved to the scientific world that she had actually floated up to the ceiling in her second body.

A vaguely similar series of experiments at the American Society for Psychical Research in New York took an amusing turn on one occasion. A number of objects had as usual been placed in a box. The box was then closed, pulled up to the ceiling, and a light turned on inside. Ingo Swann's part in the experiment was to float up to the box in his second body, peer through a small hole at one end, and then sketch what he saw.

One afternoon, Swann peered into the box and could not see a thing. This wasn't really very unusual. It often happened that he saw only darkness at first. After a minute or so, however, the objects came slowly into focus.

But this time, something seemed to have gone wrong. The inside of the box was totally dark. Although he was only supposed to peer through the hole, Swann floated into the box itself. He discovered the source of the problem as soon as he got inside.

"Hey!" he shouted. "Somebody forgot to turn on the light."

respect, he wrote. She had correctly described the objects on the table in his study and he confirmed that he had read a paragraph from Einstein's book. He also confirmed that he had sustained a head injury which required bandaging. And, yes, he had greeted Mrs. Garrett when he sensed her presence in the room.

There didn't seem to be any logical explanation for Mrs. Garrett's strange powers. She couldn't, in fact, explain them herself. She knew that she left her physical body and entered her second body, but she didn't know how she did it. Strangely enough, she wasn't even particularly interested in astral projection.

Dr. Muhl, of course, had a tough job. She was convinced in her own mind that Mrs. Garrett had somehow visited Dr. Svensen in Iceland. How she had done it, though, was a mystery which defied explanation. She had studied Mrs. Garrett closely during her out-of-the-body experience and had seen nothing out of the ordinary.

Many other scientists have been faced with exactly the same problem. They have worked with subjects who could consciously project their astral bodies to distant persons and places. Unfortunately, these projections are not accepted as fact because they have not been proved under laboratory conditions.

Until that happens, the majority of scientists will continue to look upon astral projection with a certain amount of suspicion.

18 THE CONTINUING SEARCH FOR PROOF

Astral projection is here to stay. We can be absolutely convinced of that. Although it has still not been accepted as a scientific fact, many scientists no longer regard it as something that should be swept under the carpet and forgotten. An increasing number of them believe that the study of astral projection should be encouraged in the hope of expanding human knowledge.

New doors are being opened all the time. More and more laboratories are conducting experiments on out-of-the-body experiences. Over 100 American universities and colleges now offer courses in parapsychology and psychic research. The Parapsychological Association has even been accepted as a member of the American Academy for the Advancement of Science.

Researchers are trying desperately hard to prove that astral projection is more than just a myth. The evidence submitted by thousands of people simply cannot be ignored. These people are not mere publicity seekers. Many of them related their experiences to the researchers only because they didn't dare tell them to anyone else. Friends and relatives simply wouldn't know what they were talking about.

People who are willing to discuss their out-of-the-body experiences are of enormous help to the scientists. In fact, it would be virtually impossible to continue the research without their help. Researchers are always interested in talking to people who have left their physical body. For laboratory experiments, however, they are particularly interested in those who can enter their second body at any time.

For its out-of-the-body studies, the American Society for Psychical Research depends almost entirely on volunteers. So far, there has been no real shortage of them. When the Society advertised for people who could project consciously, it received a flood of responses. One hundred of those who replied to the advertisement were invited to take part in an experiment.

The experiment was designed by Dr. Karlis Osis, the Society's Research Director. He invited 100 astral projectors to come to his office in their second bodies at a prearranged time. They were to look at certain objects on a coffee table, then report what they had seen by mail or phone. An assistant was always in the office in the hope of seeing one of the projectors in his or her astral body.

Fifteen of the 100 volunteers appear to have visited the director's office in their double. A few more claimed to have made it to New York, but then lost interest or forgot about the experiment. One was sidetracked to a burning building a block away. Another floated about in the Society's headquarters, but didn't go to the director's office. Still another projector found herself in an apartment across the street. Some people there were preparing an art exhibit and that interested her more than the objects on Dr. Osis's coffee table.

The mode of travel differed from person to person. Some merely thought of the office and they were there at once. A Massachusetts projector said that she had flown over smoking chimneys. A young woman who flew in from Toronto, Ontario, reported seeing the Great Lakes and ships in New York Harbor. Another projector recognized Louisville, Kentucky as she flew in from Oklahoma.

Several of the astral projectors were seen while in Dr. Osis's office. In one particularly interesting case, an assistant sensed that someone was in the office with her. Knowing that a Mrs. Marmoreo was supposed to arrive in her second body at that time, the assistant took a couple of flash photos of the room.

A few minutes later, the phone in the office of the American Society for Psychical Research rang. It was Mrs. Marmoreo calling from her home in Toronto. She had just been in the office in her double, she said, and there had been a woman in the doorway holding a camera. A bright light had then been flashed directly into the eyes of her double.

Hopes ran high for a time, but unfortunately, there is still no photographic proof of a second body.

Pat Price, former mayor and police chief of Burbank, California, has taken part in a number of experiments at the Stanford Research Institute. In one series of nine tests designed by Dr. Harold Puthoff and Dr. Russell Targ, Price was to locate staff members who had driven off to an unknown location somewhere in the San Francisco area.

The test rules were not at all difficult to follow. One or more members of the staff would drive to an undisclosed point and remain there for half an hour. Price would stay in the laboratory during that time. With either Targ or Puthoff in attendance, he would have an out-of-the-body experience and attempt to project to the place where the car had gone.

Price never had any trouble projecting. He would simply relax for a minute, then enter his astral body. Although no one in the laboratory knew where the car had gone, Price believes that he always arrived at the target immediately after projection.

A careful study of his descriptions, however, leaves some doubt about this. In three cases out of nine, he seems to have missed the target area. Nevertheless, the results of the other tests are certainly impressive.

There are many cases on record in which an animal has seen or sensed the presence of someone who was having an out-of-the-body experience. Crookall tells about an Englishwoman who projected frequently to her son, who lived in a lonely farmhouse on the Yorkshire moors. The son owned a large German shepherd dog which always went wild when she appeared in her second body. The woman kept forgetting that her second body could not be harmed and fear kept pulling her back into her physical self.

In time, the woman overcame her fears and the dog apparently became accustomed to her ghostly

presence. The frenzied barking gradually became a nervous growl. The growl soon became a whine and then a whimper. After a dozen or so visits, the dog actually seemed glad to see her. The son, however, never did become aware of the fact that he had been having an astral visitor.

D. Scott Rogo, author of *Mind Beyond the Body,* says that his dog often barked at him when he projected and similar instances are mentioned by other writers. In one case, a young man floated into a room where four girls were sitting. The very second he appeared, a small dog charged straight at him and began barking furiously. It seemed as though the dog actually wanted to bite him, but didn't quite know how to go about it.

Not much laboratory work has been done with animals, but Dr. Robert Morris at the Psychical Research Foundation in Durham, North Carolina, has made a modest start. He has studied animals to see if their activity changes when they are visited by an astral body. If there is a significant change, it might mean that the animal is aware of another presence in the room.

Dr. Morris's star subjects are Stuart Harary and his pet cat. The cat is normally very active. It plays happily in its cage, meowing at regular intervals. All activity stops, however, when Harary appears beside or inside the cage in his second body. At such times, the cat stays quietly in one place and doesn't make a sound.

This experiment in itself doesn't mean much, it's true, but Dr. Morris plans to continue his study of the relationship between animals and astral bodies.

Interesting as these experiments are, they have still not produced any hard, cold, scientific facts. There are simply no rules that apply in all cases of astral projection. D. Scott Rogo says, "The entire out-of-the-body experience is a kaleidoscope of contradictions and we don't have the slightest understanding why. If a man tells us that he has had an out-of-the-body experience, we have to take his word for it because it can't be proved."

It's only in recent years, of course, that the practice of astral projection has gained a degree of respectability. Before that time, it was something to be talked about in whispers or not at all. People who had left their bodies were reluctant to tell anyone what had happened to them. They were afraid of ridicule—and nobody likes to be laughed at. Even today, many volunteers ask the researchers not to use their names.

We can hardly blame them. Although out-of-the-body experiences appear to be much more common than most people think, they are still shrouded in mystery. Descriptions of the astral body and the astral world differ dramatically from person to person. Many projectors say that they simply could not tell anyone about their astral journey. They had entered a world so strange and beautiful that there were just no words to describe it.

There are a few, a very few, scientists today who accept astral projection as a reality. *Proving* that it is a reality, though, is something entirely different. "I rather suspect that we'll never know exactly what an out-of-the-body experience is until we find new ways of approaching the subject," one said, then added,

"Perhaps then we'll be able to produce convincing, meaningful data under controlled laboratory conditions."

The question still remains: Do millions of people actually leave their physical bodies behind them and travel into a beautiful new world where there is no pain or unhappiness?

That is a question which some dedicated scientists and researchers are trying very hard to answer for us.

We can only wait and see what their answer will be.

FOR FURTHER READING

Aylesworth, Thomas G. *ESP.* New York: Franklin Watts, 1975.
Baker, Dr. Douglas M. *Practical Techniques of Astral Projection.* New York: Samuel Weiser, Inc., 1977.
Bartlett, Dr. Laile. "Science Probes Beyond the Fifth Sense." London: The Reader's Digest Association, Ltd., September 1977.
Battersby, H. F. Prevost. *Man Outside Himself.* Secaucus, N.J.: University Books, Inc., 1969.
Black, David. *Ekstasy: Out-of-the-Body Experiences.* New York: Berkley Medallion Books, 1976.
Blackmore, Susan. *Parapsychology and Out-of-the-Body Experiences.* London: Society for Psychical Research, 1978.
Bord, Janet. *Astral Projection.* New York: Samuel Weiser, Inc., 1973.
Cohen, Daniel. *Dreams, Visions, & Drugs.* New York: Franklin Watts, 1976.
Crookall, Dr. Robert. *The Study and Practice of Astral Projection.* Seacaucus, N.J.: The Citadel Press, 1976.
Fremantle, Francesca, and Trungpa, Chogyam. *The Tibetan Book of the Dead.* London: Shambhala, 1975.
Green, Celia. *Out-of-the-Body Experiences.* New York: Ballantine Books, 1973.
Greenhouse, Herbert. *The Astral Journey.* New York: Avon Books, 1976.
Greenhouse, Herbert. *The Book of Psychic Knowledge.* London: Corgi Books, 1975.
Larsen, Caroline. *My Travels in the Spirit World.* Rutland, Vt.: Charles E. Tuttle, Co., 1927.
Monroe, Robert A. *Journeys out of the Body.* London: Corgi Books, 1974.
Moody, Dr. Raymond. *Life After Life.* New York: Bantam Books, Inc., 1975.
Moser, Robert E. *Mental and Astral Projection.* Sedona, Arizona: Esoteric Publications, 1974.
Muldoon, Sylvan, and Carrington, Hereward. *The Phenomena of Astral Projection.* London: Rider & Company, 1969.

Muldoon, Sylvan, and Carrington, Hereward. *The Projection of the Astral Body.* London: Rider & Company, 1968.
Panchadasi, Swami. *The Astral World.* Desplaines, Ill.: Yoga Publication Society, 1977.
Panchadasi, Swami. *The Human Aura.* Desplaines, Ill.: Yoga Publication Society, 1976.
Powell, A. E. *The Astral Body.* Wheaton, Ill.: Theosophical Publishing House, 1973.
Rampa, Lobsang T. *The Third Eye.* London: Corgi Books, 1959.
Rampa, Lobsang T. *Twilight.* London: Corgi Books, 1975.
Rogo, D. Scott. *Mind Beyond the Body: The Mystery of ESP Projection.* New York: Penguin Books, 1978.
Sava, George. *A Surgeon Remembers.* London: Farber and Farber, 1953.
Shay, Joseph M. *Out of Body Consciousness.* St. Louis, Missouri: The Lumen Press, 1972.
Swann, Ingo. *To Kiss Earth Good-Bye.* New York: Dell Publishing Co., Inc., 1975.
Wheeler, David R. *Journey to the Other Side.* New York: Grosset & Dunlap, 1976.
Wilson, Colin. *Strange Powers.* London: Abacus, 1975.
Yram. *Practical Astral Projection.* New York: Samuel Weiser, Inc., 1974.

INDEX

Accidents, 59, 61–64
Advancement of Science, American Academy for the, 105
Afton, Virginia, 77
Algonquins, 4
Amateurs, 82
American Indians, 4
Animals, 108, 110
Astral body, 47–51, 69
　　return, 15–19
Astral cord, 43–45, 48, 56
Astral Journey, 4, 63, 87
Astral Projection, 12, 34
Astral sounds, 79–80
Astronomy, 23, 25–27
Astrophysicists, 25, 26
Auras, 44, 48

Barriers, 78–79
Bible, 4
Book of Psychic Knowledge, 43
Books, 77
Brain wave patterns, 22
Breathing, 79
Buddhists, 12

California, University of, 3
Carrington, Hereward, 33, 47, 48, 53, 66, 79, 83–84
Central Premonitions Registry, 26
Children, 1–3, 87–93

Chinese, 4
Christians, 4
Clinical death, 71
Clothing, 48–51
Communication, 68, 72
Conscious projection, 12–13, 81–84
Consciousness, 79
Control, 18–19, 27
Conversations, 68
Cord-activity, 45
Crookall, Robert, 10, 15, 21, 32–33, 44, 82, 89, 95, 96, 108

Dangers, 81–85
Death, 8, 45, 71–75
Descriptions, 100, 111
Destinations, 79
Doctors, 56–59, 61, 63–69
Dreams, 37–41
Dress, 48–51
Drugs, 56
Duke University, 3, 99
Durham, North Carolina, 41

Eastern religions, 4
Egyptians, 4
Elsie, 34–35, 98
Experience of Dying, 71
Experiments, 21–23, 25–27, 39–41, 84, 100–111
　　84, 100–111

Family ties, 67
Fate magazine, 79–80
Fear, 66, 78, 85, 89, 108
Fox, Oliver, 12–13, 33–35, 81–82, 97–98
Freedom, 66
Friends, 68, 72

Gail, Mrs. Francis, 57–58
Garrett, Eileen, 103–104
Ghosts, 29–30, 32–35, 49
God, 68, 69, 72, 74
Green, Celia, 18, 44, 48, 61, 62
Green, Hughie, 61–62
Greenhouse, Herbert, 3, 37, 43, 45, 50, 63, 82–83, 87–89, 91, 98

Happiness, 72–73, 97
Harary, Stuart, 41, 110
Hart, Hornell, 3, 5
Hearing, 67
Hendry, Myrtle, 56
Higher Psychical Development, 33
Hindus, 12
History, 4
Hout, J. B., 56–57

Illness, 53–58
Indians, 4
Injury, 8, 59, 61–64
Instantaneous projection, 7–8, 12, 37, 87
Instruction, 77–80, 105

Journey to the Other Side, 74
Journeys Out of the Body, 4
Joy, 68, 73, 82, 97, 98
Jupiter, 23, 25

Kathy, 88–89
Kubler-Ross, Elisabeth, 71, 73

Laboratory studies, 99–105
Lamas, 4, 12
Larsen, Caroline, 50
Life after death, 71–75

Life After Life, 65
Light, 44, 48, 67–68, 72
Loneliness, 72, 89
Love, 97–98

Mail-order courses, 83
Mariner 10, 26–27
Measurement, 99
Mental and Astral Projection, 79
Mercury, 26–27
Mind Beyond the Body, 110
Miss Z, 101–102
Mitchell, Janet, 22, 26
Monks, 4, 12
Monroe, Robert, 4, 48–49, 77–79, 84–85, 97–101
Monroe Institute of Applied Sciences, 77
Moody, Raymond, 65–69
More Astral Projections, 32
Morrell, Ed, 8, 10
Morris, Robert, 110
Moser, Robert, 79, 83, 95
Muhl, Anita, 103, 104
Muldoon, Sylvan, 7, 17–19, 27, 44–45, 47, 66, 72, 79, 83–84, 97
  childhood projection, 1–3
My Travels in the Spirit World, 50

NASA, 25, 26
Near-death experiences, 65–69
New Testament, 4
New York, City College of, 21

Observation, 99
Oppermann, Roger, 63–64
Osis, Karlis, 71–72, 106–107
Out-of-the-Body Experiences, 18

Pain, 8, 53–54, 61, 66
Parapsychological Association, 105
Parapsychologists, 59, 82
Parapsychology, 105
Peace, 66, 68, 89
Phenomena of Astral Projection, 17
Pioneer 10, 25

INDEX

Practical Astral Projection, 97
Price, Pat, 107–108
Projection of the Astral Body, 84
Proof, 99, 111–112
Psychic research, 105
Psychical Research, American Society for, 7, 21–23, 26, 27, 71, 99, 102, 106–107
Psychical Research, British Society for, 30, 38
Psychical Research Foundation, 41, 110
Psychophysical Research, Institute of, 61
Puthoff, Harold, 25, 107, 108

Reasons, 95–98
Relatives, 68, 72
Relaxation, 78–79
Religion, 4, 10–12, 68, 69, 74
Responsibility, 15–16
Reykjavik, Iceland, 103
Ridicule, 74
Rogers, Garth, 17–18
Rogo, Scott, 110, 111

St. Paul, 4
St. Peter's Cathedral, 10–11
Sava, George, 57–58
Scientists, 99
Self-discipline, 13
Shoshones, 4
Silence, 67
Sleep, 4, 78
Solow, Victor, 74–75

Spontaneous exteriorization. *See* Instantaneous projection
Stanford Research Institute, 21, 23, 25, 99, 107
Study and Practice of Astral Projection, 10, 82
Surgeon Remembers, 57
Svensen, D., 103–104
Swann, Ingo, 7–8, 21–23, 25–27, 91–93, 102–103

Tanous, Alex, 27–28
Targ, Russell, 25, 107–108
Tart, Charles, 3, 98, 100–102
Techniques, 12–13, 77–80, 84
Thought transference, 33, 68
Time, 83
To Kiss Earth Good-Bye, 91–92

Unconsciousness, 56
Universities and colleges, 105
University of Virginia Medical School, 100

Vietnam War, 27–28
Virginia, University of, 3–4, 99, 100
Vision, 67
Volunteers, 106

Weightlessness, 66
Wheeler, David, 74
White, Carol, 87–88
White robe, 49
Wilmot case, 30, 32

Yram, 97

"That's impossible," one of the technicians replied. "I turned it on myself."

"Well, it's not on now," Swann told him.

The box was lowered and Swann was right. The light was not on.

One of the most famous and best-documented astral journeys was undertaken by Mrs. Eileen Garrett. The experiment took place in San Diego, California and was conducted by Dr. Anita Muhl. Mrs. Garrett's task was to travel to Reykjavik, Iceland in her second body. Upon her arrival in Reykjavik, she was to make contact with Dr. D. Svensen, Chief of the Division of Mental Health. Dr. Svensen had been told the time and the date of the experiment.

Mrs. Garrett took off on her astral journey from Dr. Muhl's apartment. She described her feelings and the things she saw on the way and these were recorded by Dr. Muhl and her secretary. Dr. Svensen was in his office when she arrived and she said that he had a bandage around his head. She then described various objects which he had set up on a table earlier.

Dr. Svensen sensed his visitor's arrival, looked up from his desk, and said, "Hello." He next took a book from a bookcase and read a paragraph on Einstein's theory of relativity. Every word he said was repeated by Mrs. Garrett and recorded by Dr. Muhl and her secretary in San Diego.

The entire experiment lasted only fifteen minutes. A copy was made of everything Mrs. Garrett had said and this was mailed to Dr. Svensen in Iceland. His reply came by return mail. Mrs. Garrett was right in every

ABOUT THE AUTHOR

Elwood D. Baumann was born in Saskatchewan, Canada, and is a graduate of the University of Wisconsin. After many years as a teacher and principal in schools in Venezuela and Turkey, he decided to devote all his time to writing and travel.

A man with a fascination for the unknown, he has researched and written books for young adults on *Bigfoot, The Devil's Triangle, The Loch Ness Monster,* and *Vampires,* all published by Franklin Watts.